FRAN
A Song for Banyana

FRAN A Song for Banyana

A Basadi Press book
First published in South Africa and Great Britain in 2021
Copyright © Fran Hilton-Smith 2021
All rights reserved.

No part of this publication may be reproduced by any means, nor transmitted, nor translated into a machine language, without the written permission of the publisher.
The right of Fran Hilton-Smith to be identified as the author of this work has been asserted.

Condition of sale
This book is sold subject to the condition that it shall not by way of trade or otherwise be lent, re-sold, hired out or otherwise circulated in any form of binding or cover other than that in which it is published and without a similar condition including this condition being imposed on the subsequent publisher.

Basadi Press
Johannesburg, South Africa

Front cover photo by Lars Baron - FIFA/FIFA via Getty Images
Back cover photo by Alan Whelan
Cover design by wearedeeperblue.co.uk
ISBN: 978-1-9160819-4-9

FRAN
A Song for Banyana

Fran Hilton-Smith
with
Alan Whelan

Published by Basadi Press

Dedication

To my long-suffering friends and family who have listened to all my tales throughout the years and given me endless support. Special thanks to Dara Carroll who has stood by me for over thirty-five years.

CONTENTS

PREFACE	9
TOMBOY TRICKS	12
MISS JONES	29
LESSON LEARNED	36
IN AT THE DEEP END	43
WOMAN OF JAZZ	50
HEROES	67
WIND IN MY HAIR	79
HELLO WORLD	87
BANYANA BANYANA	106
NAIJA	137
FRANCE 98	164
HIGH PERFORMANCE	172
JOIN FIFA, SEE THE WORLD	192
DOING IT FOR OURSELVES	219
ACHIEVEMENTS AND AWARDS	234

PREFACE

Anyone who looks back on their life can trace plenty of twists and turns that made them the person they have become. Many life decisions in those times when you chose the right fork in the road were often due less to sound judgment or foresight, and more to a combination of good timing and blind luck. I have had my fair share of both. I have also been in the wrong place at the wrong time, and suffered setbacks in my career when I should have been succeeding.

The remarkable course of my story has brought me to the belief that the boundaries I crossed will never be crossed again. The unique combination of living in South Africa in an era that saw the end of apartheid, the re-entry of South Africa into world sport, the formation of the South African Football Association, the growth of women's football, the relaxation of the immorality laws, greater social acceptance of gay lifestyles and the explosion of pop music since the 1960s, all coalesced into a fantastic backdrop against which I lived my life.

Playing on the stage of the London Dome with my jazz band Basadi, watching the progress of my beloved Banyana Banyana, and meeting my hero Nelson Mandela, as both coach and musician, were just some of the thrills I was lucky enough to enjoy.

The two underlying threads that have sewn the tapestry of my life were football and music, both of which brought me into contact with some remarkable people. I have had some wonderful friends and terrific colleagues with whom I am proud to have worked. While that was going on I started the first all-girl motorcycle gang in Johannesburg. Some of these milestones may seem tame by modern standards but it is important to record my experiences in the old South Africa, and how it has changed.

I am proud to be African born, as were my parents and the rest of my immediate family. Our descendants were from Europe (my father's family were from Wales; my mother's from the Netherlands), so much of my career has been spent crossing the great divide that separated the European and African cultures—of sport, music, lifestyles —and also crossing gender barriers that, in South African football at least, still exist. Thankfully those barriers are starting to come down, but during the dark days of apartheid it took all of my determination and occasional bloodymindedness to cross into a world in which, as a white and as a woman, I was not supposed to venture. On the contrary, I regularly sought out African musicians to join my bands and scouted unsung sporting talent in the townships to grow women's football.

I played in women's teams that were multiracial long before the men's game, in both white and black areas. Fellow whites (some of whom never ventured near a black neighbourhood) believed I was fearless because I would drive alone to the Johannesburg townships of Meadowlands and Orlando for football practice, or later in life as a coach evaluating future stars on dusty, makeshift pitches. But whenever I was greeted with 'Banyana

Banyana, coacha, Franzo!' I was made to feel immediately at home.

As a coach I was usually the only white on the touchline. Later as a football administrator I was often the only white and the only woman in board meetings. As a drummer, guitarist and bass player, I was normally the only European in a variety of funky Soweto rehearsal studios, where some of the locals must have thought I had taken a wrong turning from the suburbs. I could be playing African jazz in Soweto in the afternoon and a Sandton wedding in the evening. Such was the beat of my life.

Football has enabled me not only to play and coach the beautiful game but also to travel to places I never dreamt I would see (and some I hope never to see again). Visiting Ghana, Zambia, Kenya, Equatorial Guinea, Namibia and so many other African countries showed me how beautiful the continent is. During my time at FIFA I also travelled to places further afield, some where I could happily live: Victoria in British Columbia, Vanuatu in the South Pacific, and Tobago in the Caribbean are three favourites that come to mind.

Finally, I'd like to offer a brief thanks to so many magnificent people who were part of my life. I'll try not to forget to mention too many along the way.

Here's my song for my beloved Banyana.

1

TOMBOY TRICKS

My life in football can be traced back to the 1960s when I would often be found kicking a ball around the streets of Primrose, on the outskirts of Johannesburg. I don't know where the interest for the beautiful game came from. I guess you drift into sport. My dad had been a goalkeeper in his day but I never saw him play, although he did go on to be a South African veteran golf and tennis champion.

My schooldays didn't start well. I can still remember my first day sitting at a front row desk crying my eyes out, hoping someone would come to take me home. They had to call my mother to come pacify me. I couldn't understand why I had to sit behind a desk when all I wanted to do was run around, wild and free.

When I discovered football, I would happily spend all my time with the neighbourhood boys because no girls wanted to chase around a field after a ball. This wasn't evidence of an early crush on the male of the species, but rather an explicit desire to *be* a boy—racing bikes, kicking a football or swinging a tennis racquet, it didn't matter what. The same applied to indoor hobbies: I wanted to play with dinky cars; instead my parents would hand me Barbie dolls. You see my early dilemma.

I would also spend time at my ouma and oupa's house, grandparents on my mother's side, where I would always bring a soccer ball to kick around the garden, seemingly in preparation for my call-up to the national team. If I kicked the ball into Oupa's prized hedge he would come at me brandishing his walking stick. There was a park adjoining the garden where my friends and I would sometimes play, but if the football went into the hedge I would send one of them to retrieve it.

Sometimes I would sleep next to Ouma's bed on a small wooden bench known as a *riempie bankie*, complete with netted animal skin base. I could not get into the bed until my oupa was in bed cuddled up with his nightcap on. I have fond memories of waking up early each morning in the tiny room opposite the kitchen where I would get a wonderful whiff from the big pot of porridge bubbling away on the old green stove—fuel for the day's football practice and general tomboy pursuits ahead.

When I was around ten years old I found my way to a small park down the road where I met a number of new boys having a kickabout. I tagged along and was begrudgingly allowed to play in goal. I had to 'pay my dues'. Slowly I managed to infiltrate the team and started playing outfield. I had to adapt fast as some of the boys were older and stronger than me. But I had a few advantages: I was left-footed, I was fast, and I was already growing into a tall and lanky girl. I used to win all the fifty-metre races at school.

Later we moved to Driehoek, a lower middle class suburb in Germiston where the stadium of the popular local team Germiston Callies was directly opposite our house, and the place of some of my fondest childhood memories. The biggest local event was the Germiston Callies v Highlands Park match. It was all out war. When the Callies were training, soccer balls would often fly over the wall and bounce into our yard. My dad would hide them in the dustbin for us to play with later. After Callies training, we could easily gain access to the stadium, which was a great time for my friends and I to get used to the full-size pitch.

Football was only one of my consuming passions growing up. Since I can remember, I have also been obsessed with bikes—anything with two wheels. I can vividly remember, aged eight, getting my first blue bicycle with brakes on the pedals, which were great for locking the wheels and making long skid marks down the road. One Christmas five years later I graduated to a beautiful crimson Raleigh. No bike was ever perfect, so there was always room for tweaking. I was forever changing the handlebars from racing to the fashionable monkey bars and then to straight bars. Then I upgraded the pedals to steel racing clips so my feet didn't slip off, essential for speed racing because if my feet slipped off the pedals I would come crashing down on the crossbar with painful consequences.

A major part of my youth was spent riding around the neighbourhood and on what seemed like long day treks or trips out for picnics. In the school holidays from morning to night I was on my bike with all the local boys. I can't remember ever seeing any girls of my age. Perhaps, like my sister Lynda, they were indoors playing with Barbie dolls or something equally silly.

Around this time, I'm not sure why, but I became obsessed with cowboys, a fascination that lasted into adulthood. There was a cowboy serial that I used to listen to on our old wireless radio. I would race home on my two-wheeled steed to be in time to hear the latest weekly adventures. By the age of eleven I had found a new friend, Colin, with whom I would play cowboys and Indians almost every day. I don't know who was egging on who, but Colin and I got up to no good. We would build forts in our backyards and spend endless hours imagining ourselves to be out on the range, cowboy hats on and holstered cap guns on our hips. We even talked to each other in slow cowboy drawls while smoking Texan plains or Lexington 10 cigarettes. The housekeeper would regularly tell my mother that the junior cowboys had been smoking out in their fort, for which we would get a hiding.

We thought of our neighbours as the enemy so we would lay traps for them in a section of waste veld opposite the house that we imagined to be the Wild West. Locals had created a footpath through the long yellow grass that grew between their houses and some local shops. We would tie knots in two lengths of grass taken from opposite sides of the path before camouflaging them so the trap was hard to spot. This would invariably lead to some poor soul tripping on the knot and falling headlong into the soft grass. This brought much joy to two bored twelve-year-old cowboys.

Between the Post Office and the café there was a telephone booth that had a wooden door with a panel at the top where at one time there had been a small piece of glass. When we had some spare cash we would buy a handful of red firecrackers, the ones that made a hell of a racket, especially in a confined space. We would then wait for some unsuspecting neighbour to use the payphone. Once they had shut the door, we would run across the road, light the firecracker and throw it through the small window. We would then run into the adjoining café and start to innocently play the pinball machine or run up onto the building roof to peer down. Very quickly there would be an almighty bang and the person—generally clutching their now deafened ears—would run out complaining like hell and looking around for their assailants.

The cowboys also mastered the art of the 'long tickey', a small coin attached to a piece of string or bubble gum which was inserted into the telephone slot and jiggled up and down to trick it into thinking a coin had been deposited. Once proficient, you could talk all day for free!

I still have a cine movie clip made during one memorable Christmas Day at my ouma and oupa's house. The film shows twelve grandchildren (eleven girls and one boy, my brother Brendan) sitting around a dining table on the closed verandah having lunch. As the eldest, I am sitting at the head of the table. Suddenly I pull out a long-barrelled six-shooter cap pistol and brandish it around. In the group photo, true to form, all the other girls are holding dolls, but I have a holster on my hip and an imitation Colt .45. How on earth I got my parents to buy me this, Lord knows.

I moved on from backyard forts to playing cowboys and crooks or cowboys and Indians with a whole bunch of kids in the nearby forest. The cowboys were armed with pellet guns, the 'Red Indians' had to make do with bows and arrows made from darts tied to the end of a long stick. Of course, the group with pellet guns would win the battle in the forest as we could shoot further than anyone with a bow and arrow. After a boy got hit with a pellet that caused a huge welt on his leg, our parents put paid to that game. But nothing was going to stop us riding around the neighbourhood living out our dreams, fuelled by John Wayne movies and the TV series *Bonanza*.

Strangely enough, as an adult I visited Canada to see my friend Metro who was coaching football to a large group of indigenous people. He knew about my fascination with the Wild West and said he would take me to meet some real native Americans. We went to a reservation and met a tribe, chief and all, who still lived together and had retained many of their cultural beliefs and customs. I was totally in awe. I was given a woven blanket as a souvenir, which I cherish to this day. A childhood dream had come true and not a cowboy or pellet gun in sight.

Meanwhile, back in my youth, boys will be boys, and that meant me tagging along with them to explore places as far as our bikes would take us, with no concept of the dangers out in the world. The innocence of childhood.

One of our favourite destinations was Primrose cemetery where we would play in the stormwater drains next to the graves. It sounds grim but it was great fun. It was here that we found our secret place. The drain pipes were just wide enough to crawl on our stomachs as far as a T-junction, where we would turn right and keep crawling. Eventually we would emerge into a small brick room with a high barred opening. We would sit and play and look through the grill, marvelling at the gravestones. We never considered the potential danger that if it had started raining the pipes would have flooded with water and drowned us all.

Later I discovered more drains. Mom and Dad regularly played tennis in Delville, Germiston. Bored, one particular day I wandered off and discovered a manhole at my feet. Sticking my head in, I saw that it led down to stormwater drains about two metres in diameter and stretched as far as I could see in each direction, large enough to play in and create echoes as I went. One section headed towards Germiston Lake and must have acted as an overflow. I climbed down the steps that led into the pipe and when my eyes were accustomed to the darkness I noticed a glimmer of light far off in the distance. I headed towards it. As if in a fairy tale, I came upon a man sitting there all alone; we chatted and shared a cigarette. He said he lived in the pipe, which to a twelve-year-old somehow seemed an attractive proposition. For weeks after that, unknown to Mom and Dad, whenever they played tennis I would make my way down the manhole, along the pipe to the light at the end of the tunnel and meet with my secret friend. I had no fear. I never discovered who the pipe man was. I think back now and wonder, if I hadn't reappeared at the tennis courts, who would have ever found me?

As you can probably tell, I was an active kid and hated being stuck behind a desk at school. When I was in standard five at Malvern convent, my mom, who taught physical education and Afrikaans at the school, fell pregnant with my brother Brendan. It didn't stop her coming to school, which she did well into her pregnancy. I was mortified. My younger sister Lynda and I had always been told that we 'had to be good' and not to embarrass my mother. Now here she was walking around on the sports field six months gone!

More fun and games ensued whenever we spent time with the extended family (Dad had two brothers and a sister). My father's elder brother, Joe, had a son, Robin, who was a year older than me. He was the blue-eyed boy of the family and clever, certainly in comparison to me, who at that age was academically more middle path. My dad always spoke highly of his nephew and his excellent school results. As you might expect, it really got on my nerves.

Twice a year without fail we would schlep down from Johannesburg to East London to see my uncle and his family for a seaside break. My parents were not exactly awash with spare cash at the time, so staying with Uncle Joe was a cut-price way to get a family holiday.

A strange quirk of my dad's was that, days before the big bi-annual road trip to the coast, he would decide to take the engine out of the Vanguard to effect some repair or other. I could never understand why this, one would imagine, quite radical mechanical intervention had to be performed at that particular instant. There would then be a race against time to put the car back together again—even working through the night—ready for the big trek south. We would often be packing the car while Dad was still tinkering under the bonnet. Somehow, though, he always managed to get the old car running.

Cousin Robin had a sister, Kim, who was the same age as my younger sister. It was a mixture that guaranteed some fun times. Robin had a bike with a speedometer on the handlebars, with which I was besotted. It was all I wanted in life. My father was absolutely adamant that I was not getting a speedo as he knew that I would be constantly checking my speed and not watching where I was going, and end up crashing into a tree or the nearest telegraph pole.

Robin's friend, called John, lived up the road and, shame, we (or rather I) would terrorise the poor lad at every opportunity. Children have a knack of picking on the vulnerable kids. We would play cowboys and crooks, and of course John would always be the crook who had to be rounded up by the good guys and locked in the dark garage. At night, when all our folks had gone out for the evening, we would go around to John's house. We knew he would be lying on his bed reading so we would throw stones at the window and scare the hell out of him. When the folks returned home his parents would come to complain to my dad and Uncle Joe. Throw stones? Who, me?

The early sixties were a great time to be by the beach listening to... the Beach Boys. We would play their records for hours on Robin's little mono record player. I still love their music to this day. Those hours listening to *Pet Sounds* were some of the formative experiences of my third great passion: music.

One year, shortly before travelling down to East London, I got my first electric guitar and amplifier (more of that later), and of course I insisted on bringing them to show cousin Robin. My sister brought every last one of her Barbie dolls, then Dad's golf clubs and all his fishing equipment had to be squeezed in to the car. If there was any room left after that lot Mom would finally load the suitcases and *padkos*—food for the road. Off we went. We had just crossed the River Orange and landed in a place called Aliwal North in what is now the Eastern Cape, when the car packed up. Dad opened the bonnet and scratched his head. There was nothing he could do. Was it something to do with his last minute engine repair? Who knew? With insufficient tools to make a repair, my dad walked to the nearest town for help. But it was Christmas holidays and garage workshops were closed, and no parts were available. There was still another six hours driving to reach East London, so we were seriously stuck.

Dad phoned his brother for a solution. He suggested we find our way to the nearest railway station and he would meet us at the other end. We all got on the next train to the coast, which was packed to the hilt with other holidaymakers. The whole family had to share a coupe cabin for two where there was barely room for the five of us, so all our luggage and guitar, amp, dolls, fishing equipment (in other words, crap) had to be left in the narrow train passage where one of us stood guard all the way to the end of the line. Other passengers were moaning like hell as they climbed over all our stuff to get to and from the dining car. The embarrassment has never left me, which of course was doubled for a child. Scarred for life.

After what seemed like the longest train journey in Africa, we finally arrived in East London. Uncle Joe was there to pick us up in a tiny Triumph Herald with barely enough room to fit a cat in the back. He had to make five or six trips back and forth to carry all the junk to his house. He was not amused.

On arrival he magnanimously offered everyone a glass of wine and then proceeded to pour it into little shot glasses as if carefully half-filling a test tube. A bottle of wine lasted a week. To be fair, there were mitigating reasons for his frugality. My dad's mother had died when they were young—Dad was five; Joe was sixteen—which meant the next few years were tough. Teenager Joe had to fend for himself and got a job on the railways; Dad's sister was taken in by an aunt; his other brother was old enough to join the Air Force. Dad was harshly brought up in a convent run by German nuns; by all accounts it was an unenviable childhood. The strict convent regime included scrubbing floors, making beds and other menial chores, which must have forced him to see life through a prism of hardship. Whenever we drove through King William's Town (now Qonce) on the way to the coast, Dad would point out the convent and we could hear the sadness in his voice.

The sibllings' austere childhoods affected their whole lives and meant they hated waste and wouldn't spend a penny if they didn't have to. Hot dogs and hot chocolate was our cut once a week at the roadhouse—Dad refused to pay for anything more. Drive-in movies on a Friday night were a huge treat. He would hate to pay to eat in a restaurant and, only when he couldn't avoid it, would order a basic margherita pizza for him and my mother to share. When he passed on, my mother rarely ate pizza again. The only expensive meal he ever ate in a restaurant was when he misread "SQ" (subject to quotation) for "R6" on the menu and ordered an extravagant fish dish by mistake. It took him an age to recover from that.

To return to my musical ambitions, the purchase of a guitar and amp may seem a lavish expense for a childhood that was a little spartan, but there were extenuating factors—I was born into a musical family. My mom was one of the best piano players I ever heard. She could play any song from memory and entertained hundreds of people in her time, especially at the old age home where she later worked and lived into her nineties. She would probably have continued for years longer but for a fall.

As accompaniment to Mom, my dad was a fine singer and, on a good day, sounded like crooner Perry Como. I like to think that some of their talent rubbed off on me. However, my musical education had a discouraging start. Aged eight I was marched off to piano lessons at the convent... and hated every minute of it. All we did was practice scales and prepare for Trinity College of Music exams. The music teacher nun sat with a ruler at the ready, daring me to play a wrong note. Whenever the family visited friends they would ask me to play something, but I couldn't manage a note without my sheet music, and even if I had the manuscript it was always boring classical stuff, which didn't exactly fire me up. When I was twelve the old nun who taught piano passed away and I was secretly delighted. (I'm probably going to hell for that thought, but I was pleased she wasn't replaced.)

My grandparents had originally thought I would be an artist because my oupa had dabbled in painting, so as the first-born grandchild of eleven girls I was marched off to numerous art classes. Finally everyone, not least the art teacher, realised that applying paint to canvas was not my forte and the lessons stopped.

Around the time the nun with the ruler died I spotted a full-sized guitar in a shop window and, after much nagging, my Auntie Lilly bought it for me as my parents could not afford it. My own musical journey had finally begun. In common with most people who pick up the guitar at an early age, the instrument was far too big for my hands and all those strings were always out of control. To make matters worse the guitar had steel strings that gave me blisters. In later years I discovered nylon stringed guitars that made it easier for tender fingers to fret the chords. Despite the callouses on my fingertips I soldiered on. Something inside me said that this was my calling.

At the age of thirteen I took up with a 'boyfriend', Roger. He quite liked me but, unfortunately for Roger, I regarded him as a friend who just happened to be a boy. Whenever we went out to the movies my sister would have to come along as chaperone, which certainly killed Roger's embryonic passion. By high school I knew that I was not like the other girls who were always talking about boys. I just liked girls, it was as simple as that.

True to my tomboy outlook, I took up judo with an instructor who also played a cowboy in a comic book series. What a perfect combination! One weekend he invited me to go with him to film a new series. So off we went to some farm to do the photo shoot for the magazine. He and a few other actors were dressed to the nines in full cowboy gear: guns, hat, spurs, the lot, with a number of horses on hand to complete the Wild West backdrop.

I had never ridden a horse except for an occasional pony that was led around by the nose. Suddenly I was handed the reins of a huge horse and told to mount as if I was the Lone Ranger. I had no clue what to do. Somehow I managed to get on its back, took hold of the reins and imagined doing what cowboys do, that is, gallop off into the distance. Which is exactly what my horse did. He followed the rest of the charging posse and started jumping over fences with absolutely no encouragement from me. In fact, quite the opposite. By this time I had lost the reins and was hanging on to the horse's mane for dear life, praying that he would stop and put me out of my misery. He finally came to a halt under some trees where I quickly slipped off, feigned a muscle injury and managed to hitch a ride back to the ranch in a truck.

In my early teens the family moved to a farm my father had bought. He was no farmer, but decided he had had enough of being an accountant and would try his hand on the land. He bought a shotgun and every now and then would shoot passing ducks that my poor mother would have to cook. People would be invited for dinner and have to chew their way through wild duck most often filled with lead shot. I still have his shotgun. After Dad's demise I had the barrel sawn off, like in the Mafia movies.

Rather than blast them out of the sky, he then decided to breed ducks and bought fifty eggs and an egg hatcher. They failed to hatch, so he bought 100 ducklings. Unfortunately no one warned the birds about my two Alsatian dogs which ate them up during the course of a single night. Next morning they couldn't drag themselves off the ground, their bellies were so full. Dad then moved on to some more mature ducks, which developed nicely. Mom wrapped them in pastry and passed them off as "chicken pies", which she sold for years to a small shop in Germiston without a word of complaint from their customers!

My dad then tried his hand at breeding calves that needed fattening up for slaughter, but they had to be hand fed with milk powder, which soon became tiresome. Some got bloated from eating grass and I remember once having to stab a calf's stomach with a knife to release the gas. Oh, the joys of farming.

One Christmas the extended family was at our place for lunch when a lone cow wandered onto the farm. The bulls went wild with ardour and came running through the house in pursuit of the lone cow that was looking for refuge.

Meanwhile the dogs proved they were still not fully under control when one of the Alsatians bit off a calf's tail. In retaliation the calf broke a duck's leg, on which I applied a splint. Visitors to the house must have thought they were at a funny farm!

In my mid-teens I moved to St Dominic's Catholic School for Girls, a convent school in Boksburg, and graduated from judo to karate, eventually gaining my black belt. My instructor was part of the neighbourhood watch and some nights I would go out on patrol with him. I never understood how my parents allowed their precious teenage daughter to go out at night with him armed to the teeth and looking for bad guys.

My childhood obsession with bicycles, no doubt rooted in my romantic conception of cowboys out on the range, graduated to motorbikes when I reached my late teens. Of course my dad was just as adamant that I was *not* getting one. I was mortified; all I wanted was a bright red Honda 50cc. Was that too much to ask? Aged seventeen, it would have made my life complete and sent the right signals of rebellion to the convent nuns. In my dreams. My disappointment deepened when, to my horror, a girl in standard nine pitched up at school on my dream bike. She couldn't even *spell* motorcycle! I could have happily strangled her with my bare hands, I was so jealous.

I begged my dad to somehow find the money and allow his daughter on to the mean streets of Germiston on her dream machine. He wouldn't budge. My life was over—but I had a back-up plan. If I couldn't ride my own bike, perhaps I could ride on the back of someone else's. I just had to find the right biker with an empty pillion seat.

Some great family friends called the Staceys had a son, Pete, who rode a Yamaha 650cc. I instantly fell in love— with the bike, not Pete, who quickly became my best friend. Unfortunately the poor lad was keen on me for years and I really didn't feel the same depths of passion. I did try, but it just wasn't there. Anyway, he took me on numerous fun-filled trips, including one night when I talked him and his friends into taking me for a spin around the convent gardens at midnight, pulling wheelies and causing a hell of a racket. The late-night arrival of the motorcycle gang woke up all the boarders and the nuns and was spoken about for weeks afterwards. They never discovered my part in the infamous raid.

Rather than quench my thirst for two-wheeled thrills, riding pillion with Pete only fuelled my enthusiasm for bikes. My desire to own my own motorcycle was not yet thwarted.

We had a close family friend called Harry Bennett who was a great singer, having sung in a Welsh choir, and would join in the singalongs at home when Mom played the piano. Once, the great Germiston-born golfer Bobby Locke came along and joined in the fun with his ukulele. He invited my dad to play a round of golf with him, which was the highlight of Dad's life. He dusted off his wallet and prepared for the occasion by splashing out on a new club, head covers and shoes.

Anyway, back to Harry. Harry had emigrated from Wales and lived in South Africa for a number of years, but now had decided to return to the old country. He had a dilapidated little Yamaha 125cc which, knowing my obsession with anything two-wheeled, he decided to leave behind for me, much to my dad's irritation. Finally I would have a bike of my own. Of course the thing wasn't running, so I had to beg Pete to make it roadworthy, which took a lot of work. Meanwhile my dad was probably hoping he never got to the end of the repairs. But Pete managed to do it. I spent many years joyfully riding around on that machine, oblivious to the fact that my parents were fraught with worry over my safety. But I had no accidents to speak of, except once when I rode over a drunk who stepped out in front of me. He was more worried about his spilt beer than any injury I might have caused.

In contradiction to my tomboy ways there was one occasion when I tried to pretend I could be like every other girl in my class. One Sunday morning at Mass in 1970 I saw a good-looking guy in the last pew. He caught my eye because he had the most gorgeous long blond hair —and I needed a partner for the convent matric farewell dance.

The following Sunday I looked out for him. There he was once more with his rock star looks sitting in the last pew. After Mass I mustered up the courage to introduce myself. His name was Phillip; he would defintely do. I took the next step and asked him if he would accompany me to the dance. Yes! I then informed him that we would need to practice our dance routine for the event. Maybe he thought he didn't have a choice, so agreed on the spot.

Soon afterwards he came around to the little house in Driehoek and we took our first missteps on the outside verandah. As the record spun on the turntable with waltzes and quicksteps my mother and sister peered out the window at the amusing spectacle. I, however, was in another world and mostly smitten by his lovely, fashionably long hair, John Denver style. I knew my friends at the convent would be madly jealous when I arrived at the dance with him on my arm.

The day before the Saturday dance we agreed to have one last practice. As he approached the house, I looked in horror at what I saw before me. He had cut his hair; he now looked like every other boy with short back and sides. I was beside myself.

My Alsation must have shared my sentiments because as Phillip stepped onto the verandah and I reached out for a welcoming hug, the dog bit his leg, believing he was protecting me from attack. Far from having a dance practice, Phillip could now hardly walk. He made it to the matric farewell but he was still hobbling. We parted ways amicably enough soon after. I wonder if he ever grew his hair back.

With thoughts of rock star boys quickly disappearing I returned to my natural environment. Despite the time spent on the seat of a motorcycle, I was still quite sporty and harboured a dream to be selected for the provincial football squad. That was all I needed to make me happy. Around this time, 1969–70, I met a lady called Elsie Gilbert who decided to start a girls' football team. This would be the official start of my football career, and the beginning of organised women's football in South Africa. Inter-provincial football, or soccer as some of us called the game, was being played in Natal, Western Cape and later in Eastern Transvaal and Southern Transvaal. I quickly made it into the Southern provincial squad, and made the number eleven shirt my own. As a natural left-footer, tall and fast, I was an asset on the left wing. I had two specialities: I could score goals from a corner with my trademark banana kicks (eat your heart out David Beckham), and my long shots on goal from outside the 18-yard box.

We played anywhere and everywhere. On one occasion we played a curtain-raiser before a Kaizer Chiefs v Orlando Pirates game, two of the biggest clubs in South Africa even then. Kaizer Motaung, the owner of *Amakhozi*, said in passing after our game that if I had been a boy he would have signed me. Praise indeed from a terrific professional.

2

MISS JONES

I left the convent school in 1970 with two ambitions: to be a rock star and/or a surfer beach bum. Bizarrely, as a back-up plan, I decided I could drive coal trucks from Johannesburg to Witbank because this was a big money-spinner—you could make R50 per trip, which was a lot of money at the time.

My parents, however, had other ideas. Because my mother was a teacher, and without much discussion with me, they decided that I should follow in her footsteps. I was not too happy about this but had little choice. I was packed off to Johannesburg College of Education in Braamfontein for teacher training. I applied to teach high school but in the first year I contracted infectious hepatitis; in fact most of the people living on our road in Driehoek got it. It was suspected that we had all caught the infection from the milk that was delivered each morning. I was sick as a dog. I could do nothing but lie still in bed for weeks until my liver had healed. My mom was also sick and my sister Lynda was rushed to ICU with meningitis. Our house came to resemble a convalescent ward at Joburg Gen.

Consequently I fell way behind in my studies. I had previously met a lady called Margie Kietzman who was studying to teach primary school pupils and offered to bring study materials to my home, but that meant I would have to change course from high school teaching to primary teaching. Reluctantly I did so. My main subjects were biology, English and physical education.

I knew a lot of students who were staying in residence so, once I regained my health, decided that would be the life for me. Mom and Dad did not share the same thought at all. (I was still a teenager so was entitled to disagree with my parents on absolutely everything!) I had a huge fight on my hands. Finally I convinced them to let me move into student digs by agreeing to come home weekends. Of course I soon found plenty of excuses not to (although I did miss home cooking, especially Mom's lemon meringue pie).

As a soon to be lapsed Catholic—the church's indoctrination had little effect on me—I was relieved at not having to get up for ten o'clock Mass every Sunday at St Augustine's in Germiston where we attended religiously (excuse pun) come hell (excuse pun again) or high water. In any case, I used to spend much of the service dozing in the pew as the priest prattled on. The only good times were when my late brother Brendan was small—he (twelve years younger than me), my sister Lynda and I would sit in what was called a crying chapel, effectively a soundproof room where we could fool around and no one could hear us behind the thick glass. We could still see the priest at the altar while babies cried their hearts out and my brother Brendan ran around like toddlers do instead of us trying to get him to sit unnaturally still in a pew. I loved him so much.

Brendan was also special for another reason. Mum and her three brothers were keen to keep alive the family name of Olie, but my uncles only produced daughters: Uncle Leo had five girls; Uncle Oscar two girls; Uncle Dr Marinus two girls. Only my mom had a boy, and in any case he took my father's name.

Brendan grew into a lovely, handsome young man and a talented footballer, making the Eastern Transvaal team. He was very close to my parents, especially my mother, and shared a cottage with them when they ran an old age home called Alan Woodrow Park retirement village in Boksburg. By this time the family were a bit better off financially, so naturally the youngest was spoilt rotten. After school, which he passed with top grades, he joined the army for his military service. My folks were so proud that they bought him a nice car. After a night out, he was returning to the military base when he lost control of the car and hit a cement barrier. He died, aged twenty-one. The terrible thing was that my folks were not told immediately about his death, but rather a friend of my brother's read about the accident in the newspaper and called my mother to confirm it. My parents never recovered. My mother, especially, was deeply affected by his death and remained distraught until the day she died in 2017, aged ninety .

Church-going was always a battle of wills between my parents and their kids, but church services improved somewhat when Mom and Dad added musical accompaniment. My mother was brilliant at playing the church pipe organ, which was located at the back of the church high up near the roof. I would often follow her up the thirty narrow steps to get to the huge instrument. I was fascinated by the many pull stops above the keys that imitated the sounds of a clarinet, saxophone, and every other orchestral instrument. I loved sitting on the floor watching Mom's feet push the bass pedals up and down. Meanwhile, my father would lead the choir.

But those rituals, smells and sounds of the Catholic Mass were behind me now. Johannesburg College of Education (JCE) beckoned. JCE had recently built new premises in Parktown. But the problem was that the campus residence for women had not yet been completed. So a crazy decision was made to house the first-year female students in a block at the men's residence called Knockando, from where we could either walk or be bussed to the college for classes.

It soon emerged that the older male students had keys for most of the doors and regularly raided our rooms, stealing the girls' bras and undies. Next morning we would see them flying from the college flagpole. Consequently door locks had to be changed and security beefed up. Streaking was a popular pastime for the men and we had regular 'sightseeing' at around midnight. On one occasion the girls decided to run topless to give the men a treat, but they were waiting for us with fire hoses and proceeded to douse us down. We never did that again.

Despite the locks being changed and the increased security to keep the boys and girls apart, many students fell pregnant during that first term and had to leave. It was a disgrace for the JCE administration as they now realised they had made a mistake by mixing the first years with the older boys. They then pushed to get us into the new residence by our second year, which they did. I shared a room with a girl called Dot who really loved the boys, including one who surfed regularly in Durban. It gave us a great excuse to make a number of crazy, fun-filled trips down to the coast in a clapped out Volkswagen Beetle to indulge my desire to be a beach bum.

Four years later I graduated and was lucky enough to get a job at Forest Hill Primary School, teaching both physical education and academic subjects. The newly formal 'Miss Jones' taught all standards, but at one point the grade one teacher took ill and I was asked to take her class. What an experience. The little ones would all come up to my desk snivelling, sniffing and snorting like so many gurgling drains, so my first class rule was that before they came near me the pupils had to blow their noses with tissues at an empty desk specially placed for the purpose. When kids were queuing to speak to me they would sometimes wet their pants while waiting—to ask permission to go to the toilet! I made another rule that if they were desperate to pee, for heaven's sake just go.

The grade one pupils told me that Mondays were 'report back' days. That was a new innovation to me but I soon learned that it was a way for teachers to learn far more than was seemly about the children's home lives. It was certainly an eye opener. Many little children don't have a filter before they speak and tend to speak their minds, so I would be treated to 'Daddy did this' and 'Mommy said that'... shew, the things I learned about Mom and Dad would have made them blush. When they came for parents' evening they sat in front of me as if butter wouldn't melt... and I would think to myself, *If you only knew what I know about you!*

A potentially more serious episode occurred when two grade one pupils went missing from class. I looked everywhere, or so I thought, but couldn't find them on the school grounds. There was one place I hadn't checked: the swimming pool. Thank God they were there, splashing away nonchalantly in the shallow end. Never before was I so relieved to see two naughty children who had skipped class.

My friend Margie not only encouraged my teaching but also introduced me to take up the great sport of rowing, which soon became a new passion. I was soon regularly rowing at Victoria Lake Club on Germiston Lake in a coxed four: four girls rowing, one coxswain steering. I found the going tough at first, not only physically but also with my coordination; regulating my stroke with the other three girls in the boat took hours of practice to get the rhythm right.

The male team of rowers at the club gave us an old wooden ark, and just as heavy. Our first task was to sandpaper down this damn boat and then revarnish it to avoid getting splinters. It took endless weekends to bring it up to scratch, time we should have spent out on the water. Getting the old tub from the boat house onto the lake was a feat in itself for four girls. Meanwhile the guys rowed in new lightweight fibreglass four- and eight-seaters that cost hundreds of thousands of rands each.

I will always remember, with a sense of glee, one day when we were laboriously rowing our wooden crate out on the lake and the top rowing men's team came zooming past in their coxless racing boat. Without the cox they miscalculated their direction and rowed up onto a speedboat ramp that was moored in the lake for waterskiers. Their streamlined boat broke in half. We tried not to laugh out loud, but falling in water will always be funny —as long as you're not the one getting a soaking.

Rowing was extremely taxing on the body and reputed to be the cause of many heart attacks. As every member of the crew was rowing in unison, I couldn't stop for a breather no matter what pain I was going through. Some races were 500 metres, some 1000 metres, which seems a lot further when you are giving everything you've got and your lungs feel as though they are about to burst. If you suddenly felt ill or woozy you just had to grit your teeth and keep going.

Despite the hurdles, the team pushed on and were duly rewarded when we won the 1973 South African 1000-metre coxed 4 championships at Roodeplaat Dam—in our vintage boat. It was, and remains, a sporting highlight of my life.

3

LESSON LEARNED

Before my teacher training began, as a sixteen-year-old I found myself playing for Germiston Callies, the team whose footballs my father would hide in the dustbin for our use later. The team joined the Southern Transvaal league from which a provincial squad was picked (which included yours truly). Throughout the 1970s I continued playing with a lot of naturally talented women who were often ignorant of tactics, team formations and modern training techniques, so I began teaching football at colleges and schools to advance the women's game. There was a long way to go to mould these individually gifted sportswomen into a coherent team, but nobody else was doing it so I took it on.

The absurdity of the longstanding international sporting boycott against travelling South African teams meant that even though, as coach, I was instrumental in picking the Springbok national team each year, no other national team would play against us, so we merely posed for an annual team photograph while regretting all the matches we could have been playing.

Domestically though there was much to do. During the early 80s I became heavily involved in the organisational side of women's football—initially in Eastern Transvaal, now Ekurhuleni, as an administrator, then towards the end of the decade as chairlady. From outside, the men may have thought that the women's game was largely a casual kickabout more for exercise than for sport. Far from it. Of course the game was amateur in the sense that there was no money in the game (sponsorship was a pipe dream), but I was immediately impressed at how organised the leagues were—fixtures, tournaments and venues were seamlessly arranged; rules were adhered to; and games were strictly officiated. They even adopted the tradition of badged blazers for the players as a sign of pride in the team.

By the mid-80s Dara Carroll, my long-suffering life partner, by default had become public relations officer for the Eastern Transvaal football region and also took on the role of secretary. She had no interest in football before I met her, but this was the beginning of women's football in South Africa so you had to get the (unpaid) help where you could! Over the years I rose up the ranks and ended up as president of SAWFA (South African Women's Football Association), which just meant I did most of the heavy lifting with no financial reward in sight.

We held an annual inter-provincial tournament in different venues around the country: Natal, Western Province, Southern Transvaal, Eastern Transvaal and Eastern Province. Natal was consistently the best team and, apart from Western Province and Southern Transvaal sharing the title in 1976, and Western Province winning in 1982, Natal were champions every other year from 1975–1989. The Natal team was also forward thinking in the area of inclusion. Although coloured players had been embraced for some time in women's football, especially in the Western Cape, in 1989 Natal fielded the first inter-provincial black player—Jane Simba.

The men's game, however, was more cautious about multiracial inclusion. While the spotlight of apartheid remained on them, the women got on with their own thing. Perhaps when the police saw black and white female players running around on a Sunday morning they might have thought it was a 'maid and her madam' having a jol. Such were the mad times we lived through.

From these annual tournaments a national team was selected. Then in the late 80s Elsie Gilbert managed to get an invite for the women's national team to go on short tours to Sardinia in Italy. I made the squad for the third trip. Bizarrely Elsie called the team Swazilad (without an 'n')—spelling mistake? Obscure pun? Who knew? Our inclusion was most unexpected because of the boycott. But the tournament was an unofficial, non-FIFA supported event, so we managed to fly under the radar of political campaigners. Official or not, it was a big tournament featuring a mixture of both national teams and football clubs, which included the USA, Yugoslavia, Canada, the Soviet Union, Bulgaria, Czechoslovakia and AC Milan. Our nickname was the Springboks, the name of all the national sports teams under apartheid. (The only side that has kept the name in modern times is the rugby union team.)

An Italian called Franco organised the tours—I wondered at the time if it was some Mafia setup. We battled to get players due to lack of finances, and our sponsor was late in fronting the cash for the airfares so Dara had to put her house up as guarantee to the travel agency before they would book the flights. We were on our way overseas.

Elsie brought an oversized kitbag in which we believed she carried all the necessary equipment for a long tournament. We all had to take turns carrying it because it weighed a ton. What was in this thing? Anyway, we schlepped off on the long, tedious flight to Italy, only to miss our connection to Sardinia. After making ourselves as cosy as possible on the airport floor for the night—still lugging around the kitbag—we finally made it to our destination where we discovered the bag was packed with bottles of water. Like Italy had no water? There was just enough room left for one kit each and two soccer balls for training and pre-match warm-ups.

The players were put up in a series of summer beach houses that had been left empty for the winter months. The house we stayed in was beautifully furnished with a fully stocked bar. We ate like royalty—three meals of delicious pasta and pizza with wine every day. We appreciated how well we were being treated and believed we could all get used to life on the Mediterranean. Elsie had to keep a firm grip otherwise some of us could have enjoyed the good life too much, or even been tempted to stay. A walk on the gorgeous beach with the most beautiful blue sea I had ever seen was a welcome respite from the rigours of match-day preparations, and remarkable also for being the first time any of us had seen topless sunbathing, something unheard of in uptight South Africa in the early 1980s.

So off we went to our first training session wearing our one and only kit with two soccer balls between the whole squad. We made the best of what we had, but it was difficult to keep our concentration when, on the opposite field, the Canadian team were training with twenty soccer balls, cones, bibs, the full monty. The Canadian coach—ex-professional Metro Gerela—must have noticed our envious looks because he came across to our pitch and asked if we wanted to borrow some footballs. How embarrassing. He also offered us a helping hand to get ready for the games ahead, which we desperately needed because Elsie acted as both manager and coach and we had no other staff. Metro also attended to all our medical needs as the injuries took their toll throughout the tournament.

From such circumstances great friendships are made: Metro and I subsequently became lifelong friends. (He came out to South Africa to help me coach the national team in 2000, and subsequently applied for the same job. He got the contract but SAFA's CEO, Raymond Hack, never brought him over. I never discovered why.)

Anyway, back to the tournament. We headed off to our first game: South Africa v the Soviet Union. For some reason, in those days just the name of the country filled me with trepidation, and now we would face their senior team on a soccer field. And what a soccer field. The pitch was impacted sand topped with gravel, surrounded by a high wall. Lord almighty. This was going to be a challenge and we hadn't yet kicked off. Commensurate with my worst fears, the Russian team were very physical, very tall and very strong. We were overwhelmed. On top of which we were slipping and sliding all over the sand. Then our prospects took a turn for the worse. Our goalkeeper was letting in goals like a sieve, and when we asked what was wrong, she said that she couldn't see under the floodlights because of the glare on her contact lenses. She had to come off; guess who had to go in goal? Little old me was now the only thing that stood between the might of the Soviet first team and a notable thrashing.

Not familiar with goalie techniques—parries, catches, saves, etc—late in the match I tried to block a fiery shot from a Russian striker but only managed for the ball to bend my thumb unnaturally backwards, inflicting a sharp jab of pain. Now I had to carry on playing with one hand.

The score was so one-sided I decided to forget the result. The opposition taught us a lesson that day in how not to prepare against more organised, fit, well-trained players. The other two games were equally mismatched; lesson learned, we returned to South Africa to lick our wounds and try again.

Some time after the tournament, one of our players was planning to go abroad on a family holiday so she applied for her R20,000 annual overseas allowance, a restriction designed by the paranoid government to prevent currency leaving the country. Strangely, she was told that her allotment had already been applied for that year—by someone else. The mystery was solved when it was discovered that the tournament organiser, Franco, was using our team sheet to smuggle money out of the country. Consequently he faced some serious legal problems and, of course, the overseas tournaments stopped.

In 1980 I moved to Eastern Transvaal where I played provincial football for ten years. I was selected for the national team but it meant little because South Africa was still suspended from FIFA, a situation that covered most of my playing days. We were readmitted to FIFA in 1993 but by then I had moved on to coaching and football administration, so I never had the opportunity to face legit foreign competition on the pitch.

During South Africa's sporting wilderness years I formed a number of amateur teams, the two most memorable being Champions and Camel's Back, named after two hangouts I frequented. At night my band (I shall soon come to my musical life) regularly played at two gay clubs: one in Braamfontein on a Friday night called Champions and another on Louis Botha Avenue on a Sunday called Camel's Back.

I was equally keen on both football and music and had no qualms about mixing the two for mutual benefit. During one gig Dara went around the club and asked numerous, probably intoxicated, ladies if they were interested in playing soccer. If they did not express absolute horror at the suggestion, she took their names and numbers. Next morning she woke them up, reminded them what they had agreed to, and told them to come to training.

So began an exciting time in my life. Some of the girls were absolutely useless at football, but boy could they party. About thirty of us would go away for weekends and what fun we had. It was a terrific time to make more lifelong friends. One, Sandy, had friends who ran a trout farm in Dullstroom, Mpumalanga, and we would all troop off there with our tents for some wild weekends, fishing for trout, drinking copiously, playing loud music, and braaing up a storm. We didn't catch much fish but these were some of the best times of my life. We also started an annual tradition of coming to my house to watch the English FA Cup final. Bets would be placed and much screaming and shouting was heard in the neighbourhood on that Saturday afternoon in May.

Despite the unpredictable quality of our team's football, we played in many tournaments, sometimes organised by the hotel group Holiday Inn in out of the way places like Newcastle, KwaZulu-Natal or Harrismith in the Free State. These tournies were another excuse for a great party and a little football. At the first tournament my crazy biking friend Bernie shot a hole through the roof of the hotel because some guys were irritating her (she was easily riled, to say the least). In the following year's programme they added a line in bold which read, "No guns allowed". Women's football!

4

IN AT THE DEEP END

Returning to my early days in teaching, I left Forest Hill primary and moved to Edenvale High School where I would remain for the next twenty years, during which time my life in amateur football continued.

At Edenvale I was more at ease teaching an older class of unruly children and establishing myself as 'Miss Jones' or as the students occasionally called me, 'Mam'. My subjects were biology and physical education, although my skills were spread quite thin once I was taken on permanently. After the end of apartheid in the early 1990s I was pleased to see model C schools go multiracial, which made for interesting times in phys. ed.

In the first year I took a group of girls swimming, which included the new intake of half a dozen black students. Before they entered the water, I asked them all if they could swim. Everybody shouted 'Yes!' or nodded profusely, keen as they were to get in the water. They all lined up on the side of the pool.

IN AT THE DEEP END

'Okay, all in!' I called. 'Let me see what you can do.'

They all dutifully jumped in and... sank to the bottom. The majority of the girls could not swim a stroke. They were splashing around like infants having their first bath and making the unmistakeable sounds of a class of girls drowning. I dived in and quickly picked them out of the water one by one. Clearly they had been told by their parents to answer 'Yes!' no matter what their teacher asked. Why I assumed they could all swim when swimming pools in the townships were as rare as Joburg snow, I just don't know. It taught me a big lesson. From that point on, new swimming groups had to gently enter the water in the shallow end to see if they could at least float before they tried a few strokes.

Schools were filling up rapidly during these early years of racial mixing, which was great for the new intake who had access to better facilities, but their arrival coincided with (or caused) a new problem—many long-established white teachers left. Consequently I was asked to take subjects I was not qualified to teach because phys. ed. was not seen as a priority.

I was then asked to take the typing class, girls only, with the old clickety-clack manual typewriters. We later progressed to electric. Computers were huge things in those days and only available to the privileged few. Luckily I had taken the subject in school so I had a passing knowledge of touch typing. Then the woodwork teacher died unexpectedly and the boys were sitting around doing nothing for that period. I approached the school principal and asked if the boys could join my typing class. His reply was suitably antiquated, even for then: 'Oh no, that's for girls.'

A popular movie at the time was *All the President's Men*, which featured male newspaper reporters who broke the story using... *typewriters*. He got the message. I won the battle and the boys came kicking and screaming to the typing class.

Considering how ubiquitous computers became within a few years, I hope the boys now appreciate having learned touch typing with me. In fact, I am positive some do. I left teaching about twenty-five years ago but still bump into old pupils in the street—usually men—who say things like, 'Mam,' (whenever someone starts a conversation with that word, I know it's a past pupil) 'you taught me typing and I am now director of a computer company.'

When I was asked to teach standard six science I knew they were getting desperate. Science, maths and accountancy were not my forte, in fact I was, and still am, pretty useless at anything involving numbers. Now it was my turn to kick and scream (politely) but I was eventually talked into taking the class. I was so unsure of the subject that I had to try out each science lesson at home the night before class to at least get a passing acquaintance with the subject. In effect I was only a day ahead of my pupils. Some classes would have a know-all who—horror of horrors—had a chemistry set at home and could prove everything I said was incorrect, or at best scientifically questionable. I did my best to negotiate around those distractions with a straight face and asked sternly that he stop interrupting my lesson. Luckily I was never caught out.

I bluffed my way through science too well, because then the principal asked me to teach matric accounting. It was getting worse. They were really scraping the barrel when they asked someone who added up on her fingers to teach accounting. The subject teacher had left in the middle of the year and everyone was panicking for the final exams. Fortunately at the time my parents were staying with me and my dad, my saviour, was a chartered accountant. Like the science classes (but this time with my dad looking over my shoulder) every evening I would have to prepare the lesson for the next day. I would try to predict what the students might ask me in class, and probe my dad for the answers. He was a good teacher; in fact he should have taken the class. It went pretty well and I never got caught out with difficult questions.

When the matric results were announced, we were all amazed to see that they showed the class had all done exceptionally well and the school got the highest marks ever in accountancy. I was suddenly flavour of the month. I realised that because I was necessarily teaching at a basic level of comprehension similar to my own, even the weak pupils were able to follow the lesson. I wish I had someone who taught more like me when I was at school because it had often seemed that whatever my maths, science and accounting teachers said went straight over my head.

As I mentioned earlier, one of my childhood ambitions was to be a rock star (I hadn't yet given up) so every year at school I organised an end of term musical. My favourite show was *Joseph and the Amazing Technicolour Dreamcoat*, which we performed with a live band. I played guitar, my friend Linda Raulstone played drums and teaching colleague Okie Fernandes played bass. Even though it indulged my love of performing and was a good way of getting to know the pupils on a creative level, the shows were only a brief respite in a job that was taking its toll on me and my colleagues.

Classes at school were now reaching forty pupils per session, eight sessions a day. Consequently teachers were opting out of the profession at a rate of knots because the pay was poor and the workload becoming too great. I never understood how such a vital service was not better paid. Teaching wore me down but I had to stick it out for the full twenty years so that I could clear my housing bond, which had been arranged through the profession.

This scheme was both a great benefit to teachers who were starting out and also something of a gilded cage because if you left before the bond was paid off, there were huge interest penalties to pay. Teachers who left the profession early were paying off their loans at a higher rate of interest for years to come.

Shortly before I resigned, I taught matric biology, a subject I felt better equipped to teach. Inevitably if you put a class of teenagers in a room and open a biology text book, one subject is bound to raise its ugly head: sex. Sex education was not formally taught at school because the powers that be decided it was a subject best left to the parents. By the number of pregnancies every year in all standards, it was obvious that many parents were neglecting the subject as assiduously as the school. I talked openly about the subject with pupils and encouraged them to ask any questions they wanted, and tried to answer as best I could. I knew that some parents would come and complain about the candid nature of the classes but I didn't care by that stage, I was leaving anyway.

Sexuality was a subject that not only concerned a group of growing teenagers, but also their temporary biology teacher. I was always scared that the school would discover my sexuality. In the 1970s teachers were fired on the spot if found to be gay, probably because they thought we would be a bad influence on the children. Consequently I had to be on my guard and always lived far from the school in case my home life was uncovered. No doubt there were other gays at school, but for the most part my colleagues could chat openly about their personal lives. I had to keep mine hidden. Gay rights were finally recognised under the new South African Constitution in 1996.

Back in the 90s I remember one incident when my soccer team went away for a boozy weekend. We had booked all the bungalows in the resort except one. All the girls were fooling around and drinking, letting their hair down and partying late into the night. The next morning I looked out the window and was horrified to see the last hut had been occupied by a group of my matric students. I quickly packed up all my stuff and snuck home. Some of the pupils must have spotted me because on Monday morning they asked if I had been at the resort with a rowdy group of women. I flatly denied it and said it must have been my sister who looked just like me (she didn't).

For the record, I also married and divorced (a man) during my teaching years. For many reasons, that is a topic best left for another day...

So my teaching career came to an end and I was looking forward to putting all my energy into football and music. I can't say that I ever had a passionate vocation for the profession but I suppose my teaching years had its moments, and it certainly beat driving a coal truck to Witbank.

But there was to be a postscript to my days in the classroom. A year after I left I was begged to help out at Bedfordview High School, a seriously short-staffed technical school for non-academic kids. I was not keen on returning to the blackboard but once again was talked into teaching typing and business economics. The kids, most of whom were bussed in from Soweto, were an unruly group to say the least and teachers battled to control classes. Unruly and unacademic they may have been, but that was no excuse for trying to push a teacher out of the window, which they did on one occasion.

I had to come up with a life-saving plan, and quick. There was a rugby field at the school so I asked the Afrikaner principal, who was a big rugby fan, if I could start some soccer teams. He fell for it, but we had to put up the corner flags and mark out the pitches ourselves. Both boys and girls were excited and we all got involved in the pitch preparations. After a few training sessions we entered teams in both the boys and girls school leagues. Now I could exercise a little power over my fractious class, which was in danger of turning into organised crowd control. The deal was that if the boys wanted to play in my soccer team they had to behave and do their homework. It worked like a bomb. Other teachers looked on in astonishment at how disciplined my classes had become.

At the end of the school year I retired again from teaching, this time for good, and concentrated all my efforts on football and music.

5

WOMAN OF JAZZ

Returning to my teenage years, as I have already stressed I had a number of competing interests as I looked forward to life as an adult—and enjoying every one of them. I had judo and karate (both fuelled by a desire to improve my personal security), I was playing regular football for the Germiston Callies, and I had an electric guitar and a loud amp. Look out world!

Then I met Leon Erasmus who would become a big part of my musical life. I learned a few guitar chords and we started a band with two more friends: Phil on bass and Jimmy on drums, and rehearsed a few Rolling Stones songs and some original material. Leon called the band Harlot, God knows why. Somehow we landed a regular gig at the Germiston 20th Century Bio, torturing moviegoers during the interval of the Saturday matinee. We played chaotic versions of songs such as "Paint it Black" at 100 mph as if we were desperate to get out of the place. The patrons were probably glad the interval was only twenty minutes long.

A friend of Leon's, an Afrikaner, came to the movie house one Saturday—not to watch the movie, but to listen to us. We braced ourselves for a barrage of criticism following our performance, but instead of a brutal assessment of our Stones covers he asked us to play at his wedding. I thought, *Are you crazy?* I had deep reservations about the invitation and kept warning Leon against the idea, which I was sure would end in tears. I felt there was a glaring mismatch between "Can't Get No Satisfaction" and a polite Afrikaner wedding. But Leon looked at the gig as a big opportunity for exposure. We agreed a fee and were booked; well, we were cheap.

Not to put too fine a point on it, the gig was an unmitigated disaster. The wedding guests were turned off by our wannabe rock star poses and began requesting traditional Afrikaans songs, which we could not play. As people got more sozzled, one guy came up to me and said he would pay R50 for us to play just one song that he knew. It was a challenge we couldn't meet. Guests continued to drink copious amounts of booze—until the bar ran dry. An Afrikaner wedding without beer is like a braai without meat, kind of pointless, so the prospects of a harmonious end to the gig looked in some doubt.

Then some bright spark spread a rumour that the band had drunk all the alcohol. In fact we were all stone cold sober, but the guests would not listen to reason. Tempers flared as the guests looked for retribution; one guy kicked in the bass drum. We hastily packed up all the gear and made our exit. We were chased out of the venue carrying half the equipment on our car roofs because the 'roadie' with the gear trailer had left the venue and was planning to come back much later. That taught us a lesson. Choose your gigs wisely.

In the early 1980s Ian Thirtle, recently arrived from England, joined the band on bass guitar, which turned the group into a fully fledged, and loud, rock band, and meant we could now play festivals. Leon had a penchant for guitar effects pedals, sometimes called stomp boxes, that distorted his guitar sound like his heroes. He used to string the pedals together in series, but if one of the batteries packed up it cut the entire signal. Result? No sound, which most often happened when he was about to break into a stirring lead solo. Later he switched to keyboards.

The band made more progress when my then partner Virginia joined on keyboards and Linda on drums. We were now called Kamikazi—well, I preferred it to Harlot. The new name allowed us all to get dressed up in suitable regalia such as Japanese headbands and lots of garish glam rock make-up. We decided to play all original material, most of which Leon, Linda and I wrote, and the gigs went down well to a hip crowd. All the practice and band rehearsals meant that by this time I was becoming quite proficient so started giving music lessons to supplement the fees from the gigs and my meagre income from teaching.

In 1982 I got the idea to form an all girl band called Chix. Leon was demoted (we told *him* it was a promotion) to sound engineer, and we found a sublime singer called Lynne Oddy and added Dot, my college roommate, on bass guitar. We then all moved into a rented house in Malvern, Johannesburg, so we had most of the band together. We decided to convert a storage room under the house into a music studio, so we collected egg boxes and bought lots of felt carpet to soundproof the walls. Virginia's daughter Carla was an infant at the time and her room was directly above, so she was rocked to sleep every night by rock music rehearsals.

It was here that I first met Dara Carroll. She was the nursing sister for the local doctor where we took the infant Carla when she was sick. I invited Dara to come and watch the band play and she soon became a firm fan of the band (and me), and followed us to numerous gigs. We were all settled and happy, but then in 1984 the landlord decided to sell the house. We were distraught, the house was perfect and the band was just getting off the ground.

I got my mom to ask estate agents she knew in Germiston to quickly find us another place, which I planned to buy. We went along for a viewing and saw a beautiful big house with a huge sunken lounge and wooden ceilings. We loved it. The only trouble was that I couldn't afford to buy it on my teacher's salary. I convinced the seller to rent it to me, but only if I agreed to his proviso that I allow prospective buyers entry to view the property.

That could have spelled disaster but he wasn't going to get rid of me that easily. Whenever the estate agent would arrive with potential buyers we would set the big ridgebacks off their leads to chase them away. It worked. Finally the owner put his foot down about our uncooperative tactics and I managed to talk him into selling the house to us at a musician-friendly price. I applied for a loan from the education department and my folks lent me the balance, which I paid back monthly.

Now the band could stay together in its own place. In later years Ian and I built a recording studio in one of the outhouses. In some ways the new house was more convenient than the old. For one thing the neighbours were now far enough away that we didn't have to soundproof the walls with egg boxes. Virginia and I split up and Dara replaced her in my affections. Dara and I are still living in the house thirty-five years later.

Incidentally, even though I had three live-in relationships with women while my parents were alive, I never 'came out' to them. I suppose my attitude was, what was the point in trying to explain to people from another generation what was so evidently in my genes. My lifestyle was apparent for all to see. They knew I was happy and getting on with my life, that was enough.

By now Chix were getting plenty of gigs. We played at a popular club called Plumb Crazy as support band to Ballyhoo, a big-name band at the time, and also supported the great Cindi Alter at the Milpark Holiday Inn. Her band Clout were probably SA's hottest ever all girl band who made it big with a song called "Substitute", which is still a radio favourite. Our longest running regular gig was at the Sandton Holiday Inn. Our singer Lynne was a big draw because of her brilliant voice; later, she cut her own LP. Meanwhile Linda was teaching me to play drums so that I could swap instruments as the occasion demanded.

Chix then entered the 1984 Battle of the Bands. Dot had recently been offered a job in Zimbabwe so couldn't take part in the competition; in her place we enlisted Debbie Lonman of Little Sister to play bass. The rearranged personnel was a good omen because we walked away with first prize. I look back at some of the songs I wrote—"Leatherman", "Standing on the Edge of Time", "Kamikazi", "Rebel" and the co-written "Money"— and still feel proud of my efforts. I believe we played damned good on the night, but what gave us an edge over the competition was that we created homemade videos, which were played on the backdrop as we performed. For instance, for the "Leatherman" video we enlisted the help of some of our male biker friends and the Chix rode pillion while waving at the camera. My biker friend Bernie was dressed up as a traffic cop (which she had once been) and played like she was issuing tickets and arresting us for road traffic violations. The more we rehearsed the scene the drunker she got; eventually she was popping wheelies in the road as well. We spent most of the day filming in the street outside my house, which prompted the neighbours to call the actual police for the disturbance—real rock star stuff. For the song "Money" we all sat around playing Monopoly with real money, occasionally throwing it in the air with abandon.

Part of the winning prize was a TV slot, a recording opportunity and a bit of cash. We were also offered a contract by an influential music agent, but that's when the whole thing started to fall apart. (How many times has that happened to a band on the brink of stardom?) Musical ability alone is never enough. The bigshot agent insisted we dress a lot more provocatively, essentially like a bunch of Houghton hookers, but that was never going to happen with this group of women. Debbie was not keen to sign the contract as she had her own band with her sister, and Linda refused to wear revealing clothes, so she left the band.

Chix slowly met its demise because we could not find a replacement drummer. I still believe that our original music was way ahead of its time; in a more progressive country like America or the UK we could have been famous. After Chix imploded, Lynne and I continued playing as a duo—Duo Tone was one unoriginal band name we employed—at weddings and company functions. We did pretty well over the next few years.

I then started a recording studio with the English bass player Ian Thirtle, who turned out to be a terrific guy with the appropriate nickname 'Spirit'. We became great friends and he moved in to my house. While staying with me, he fell in love with a black woman, a famous singer whose name I won't mention. She also came to stay in the house for a while, although that simple act fell foul of the apartheid law called the Group Areas Act that made it illegal for different races to mix—which included a black woman living in a white neighbourhood. It was a constant worry for all of us as she had to sneak in and out of the property hoping a white neighbour wouldn't spot her, made worse by the fact that a police colonel lived next door. If she was spotted by an inquisitive neighbour we had to pretend she was our maid. It was an appalling environment in which to conduct a love affair. When she left him, Ian was inconsolable.

Later, in August 1988, on his ride to the recording studio, Ian had a serious motorbike accident and died from his injuries. I was devastated and sold up the studio. I miss him to this day. In his honour the last band I played in with Lynn and John Goodenough was called Spirit 2.

Around this time I met a lady called Bernie (not to be confused with my gunslinging biker friend). She had met my mom professionally through her social work in Boksburg, and mentioned her desire to learn to play guitar. I was happy to take on another pupil. Shortly after the lessons began, Bernie got us a Friday night gig in a seedy hotel on the wrong side of Boksburg North. Her playing was coming along nicely so she joined the band for the show. As soon as I walked into the venue I could tell it was the sort of dingy place where local tradesmen and manual workers came to forget their troubles by spending their hard earned money on booze. We were only paid R50 for a four-hour gig: 8 p.m. to midnight. It was going to be hard work.

But then a strange thing happened. Bernie was a beautiful, sexy girl with long black hair who wore the shortest ever mini-skirts. The guys in the audience wiped the fug out of their eyes and turned their attention towards her. I noticed some men were so besotted that they started stuffing money into the sound hole of her acoustic guitar. They probably just didn't want the set to end and wanted more time to gaze at the winsome guitarist. We could have played the national anthem all night and they would have been just as happy. We made far more money out of Bernie's guitar than we ever earned from the landlord.

We then moved to an even seedier hotel in Benoni called the Prospector (more fool's gold!) for another Friday night gig. Poor Dara was dragged along to act as the sound engineer. She needn't have bothered. The hotel was a pick-up joint filled with people who couldn't have been less interested in the sounds emanating from the band. It was strange to be playing innocent pop songs on stage while watching hookers soliciting customers. One night after the gig we carried our gear out to the car park and noticed a sedan parked in front of my car. As I put on the lights, three tiny heads popped up from behind the seats. I realised that while their mother was trying to make a living inside the hotel, these three children were locked in a car outside in what passed for Benoni childcare.

What with my progress in the disciplines of judo and karate and under the influence of my vigilante instructor, I was taking more seriously the subject of self-protection, especially after those gigs in bars we shouldn't have played. The law of averages suggests that it was inevitable I would face a dangerous situation at least once during my clubland forays. One night I was at a popular nightclub with my brother Brendan, sister Lynda and her husband Billy. Brendan by this time had become a proficient kickboxer, and of course I was by now a black belt karate instructor, so we thought we were invincible. Billy was also handy with his hands.

Some ladies were dancing in a group and asked a lone chap to join them. He wasn't keen but they were insistent. He gave in and joined them on the dance floor. Suddenly a gang of the girls' male friends arrived, all armed to the hilt with guns, who were not too happy about this hapless guy seemingly making moves on their girls. To show his displeasure, one proceeded to smash a beer bottle and stab the man in the throat with the jagged edge. We were all powerless to help.

That was the moment I decided to get a gun and got one for my brother too. In for a penny, I thought, and bought myself a powerful Astra Magnum .357. We all went for shooting practice and it turned out I was a bit of a sharpshooter! In the late 1980s crime was rising inexorably in Johannesburg so I wore the gun wherever I went, first in a shoulder holster and then on my hip. Thank God I never had cause to use it in anger but it certainly instilled a degree of confidence and made me feel protected in some potentially dangerous situations.

When the political climate worsened, we thought we wouldn't be able to buy bullets, so I bought my own pistol loading kit. But once I got it home I was concerned that I might add too much gunpowder and blow my hand off, so I usually put in too little and the lead bullet would plop out. I soon gave that up as a bad job.

Bernie and I upped our game as a duo and moved to Champions bar where all the soccer girls of mine hung out. The regular crowd liked us so much that we played a residency for nearly a year. Bernie then fell pregnant; even so, she continued to play. She called me one Friday morning to say that she was in labour and I would have to play alone. Baby born, Bernie was soon back in action. The show must go on!

Things then took a devastating turn. Our ex-singer Lynne Oddy was diagnosed with cancer and went through hell. I was deeply affected by watching her being subjected to all that chemo, which lasted for years. The rest of the band were all traumatised too. She died in August 2000. A good buddy gone too soon.

In the 90s I went on to play with another great musician who brought along his fair share of personal problems. Mervin Du Toit was a wiz at computerised music and put down all the backing tracks we needed for each gig: brass, bass guitar, guitar, whatever was required. Calling ourselves Bonnie and Clyde, Mervin and I played wedding and corporate gigs, despite his weakness for the demon drink. His drinking got so bad that one night during a gig I suddenly realised he was playing the wrong song—he had drifted off into a world of his own and was playing along to a different soundtrack in his head. I had to put my foot down after that.

One evening we were playing a show with a bigger band when my friend Sandy arrived. She had never seen us play and had not met my new band member. Mervin, stationary at the best of times, always wore sunglasses on stage—the rock star look probably helped hide his bloodshot eyes. Sandy saw a non-moving man wearing dark glasses playing guitar and for some reason decided that he was blind. Perhaps she was thinking of Stevie Wonder. She must have had a glass of sherry too that night because she started pulling funny faces and gyrating in front of him. When we had a break Mervin stepped off the stage and Sandy collapsed in a heap as she realised he wasn't blind after all.

Playing weddings was traumatic enough without worrying if Mervin was able to focus or not, or even play the same song as the rest of the band. I was also constantly worried that an amplifier would blow or the mixing desk pack up. We could hardly tell the happy couple to come back next week for a retake. I was always relieved when those events were done and dusted. Looking back, it was always me who took the responsibility for the success of the gigs, even though my plate was already full with soccer matches and teaching duties. This led to stress and perhaps held me back in certain situations that otherwise I should have grabbed with both hands. I guess I was a worrier.

I believe Mervin lived a chaotic lifestyle because he died under strange circumstances. One night he got beaten up at a pub, after which he just about managed to make it home. He spent many days in bed apparently recovering, but his elderly mom and aunt didn't realise how badly he was hurt and he passed away from his injuries.

I played with many different line-ups during the 1990s, including a five-piece called Freeway. Then I joined John Goodenough and school friend Phil to keep Spirit 2 alive as a three-piece rock band that played a lot of ZZ Top. I played drums, which was physically draining. Actually I was exhausted after every long gig. John took on most of the vocal duties and the audience used to love his version of "Keep your Hat On".

We were attracting bigger crowds to our gigs but our dream was to play at *the* rock club, Dylan's in Rocky Street, Yeoville. If you got a gig there you were made. It was where all the local music connoisseurs hung out and demanded that the songs be played exactly as written and sound as close as possible to the original. We rehearsed until our fingers bled. It paid off; finally we got a gig. We were all so excited—until we found out the time slot: 2–5 a.m., Sunday night into Monday morning. My heart sank as I was still teaching at the time. Still, how often do you get a chance to play at the top club in town? We *had* to do it.

As the date of our first show approached, I felt a bit more relaxed about the audience as I got to thinking, *How many people are going to show up at 2 a.m. on a Monday morning?* I was so relaxed that I dozed off on the Sunday evening and the alarm clock didn't go off. At nearly two o'clock John phoned me to find out where I was. I still had to pack up the drum kit and drive to Johannesburg from Germiston. When I got there I was amazed to see the place packed to the rafters. On a

Monday morning! It turned out that Dylan's was an after-hours haunt for all the artists and waiters from other clubs and theatres throughout the city. We had to lug the drums in the front door and rather embarrassingly carry them over the heads of the punters to the stage. Despite the audience having to wait impatiently until we were set up, the gig went well and we got paid R50 each. After the gig, John put his pay down on the bar for a bottle of whisky in an act of both relief and celebration. I rushed home, showered, jumped into the car and taught a full day at school.

We kept up this punishing schedule for about three months before the regular gig ended, but we were proud that we had achieved our goal of playing Dylan's. I was exhausted, especially as around this time women's football was under threat from the underhand tactics of the newly constituted South African Football Association (SAFA), which led to the High Court, a situation that I shall explain in a future chapter.

By now Leon Erasmus was running a number of rehearsal and recording studios in Newtown, downtown Joburg, a great place to practice and meet other musicians. I often saw Brenda Fassie and her entourage arriving in an open-top VW Golf packed with supporters and copious amounts of booze. One day, around 1998, I happened to be visiting the studios and heard three black ladies from Soweto playing some terrific jazz. They turned out to be Mabatho on flute, Zanele on clarinet, with another lady on keyboards. They said they had trained overseas with the London Philharmonic Orchestra, which certainly impressed me. There was a set of drums in the room so I asked if I could jam with them. They all looked askance at this white woman muscling in on their vibe, but agreed. I didn't know any of the songs they were rehearsing so I just followed the beat to what were mostly traditional African jazz tunes like "Pata Pata", "Lakushoni

Langa" and "Siwelele". We jazzed up the songs and gave them a dance beat. After a while they could hear that I was really into the music. We talked and jammed some more. Later, Mabatho's sister Dineo joined us on bongos.

Soon after, Basadi Women of Jazz was born, and Mabatho even had a manager who secured us the occasional gig. She and I came up with the name (Basadi means women in isiZulu).

We moved out of Leon's practice rooms to the famous rehearsal studios at Dorkay House off Eloff Street, a run-down building that was a refuge for black musicians who plied their trade during apartheid and where many top bands came to practice: Hugh Masekela, Mahotella Queens and Dorothy Masuka, amongst others.

It was here that I met Vangeli (strange name; brilliant musician), who would feature large in my musical life for years to come. The gifted Vangeli Dlamini could play *any* instrument with ease. He was not only naturally talented but also a real, well groomed gentleman who was always smartly dressed while those around him usually wore casual clothes. I was keen to get Basadi off the ground but first we needed to find a female bass guitarist, which was harder than it sounds. While we searched, Vangeli taught me some bass riffs for the songs in our repertoire, the way African jazz was *meant* to be played. Even though I had studied classical piano and could read music, he instructed me without music sheets, and taught me how to feel the rhythm. He was a natural teacher.

The sound of the band was soon grooving with me on bass so we then turned our attention to looking for a drummer, which we found in Lilly, and enabled me to move permanently to bass duties. The last piece in the jigsaw was to find a keyboard player to complete our all girl outfit. Impossible. Our dilemma was that Vangeli was so good on keyboards that he became a crucial part of our sound and any potential replacements suffered by comparison. He had such a great feel for the keys and a gentle, passionate touch that I came to realise in my heart of hearts—even though I wanted another all girl band—he was impossible to replace.

We often practiced in the depths of Soweto, which was convenient for the rest of the band but a little risky for me to be driving alone in the township late at night. On gig days I used to pick Vangeli up from neutral points in the township or else he would emerge out of a dark doorway to meet us. We were not invited in. I was never exactly sure where he lived but I guessed he lived a humble life, despite always being well turned out. No matter what his home life was like, at the show he would play like an angel, usually bent over with his nose to the keys, absorbed in the moment, somehow making us all sound better than we actually were.

Even though there was no shortage of great singers in Joburg, we struggled to keep decent female vocalists for any length of time; they came and they went, showing no real commitment to the band. How difficult was the gig? They didn't have to lug instruments around and set up the PA and drum kit before the sound check or dismantle it all afterwards; they just pitched up to a show and sang their hearts out. Dragging instruments around the city was always a pain, which is one of the reasons many bands fail, but I took full responsibility for that so I expected nothing more from the others—I just wanted them to show up and play beautifully.

Despite the revolving door of singers in the band, Basadi was cooking. We now had a sizable following of fans, which probably explains why we were invited to play a number of huge open-air festivals. Often older, sceptical black men would come up to me afterwards and claim that it couldn't have been me playing the bass, that it must be a recording because it sounded so like the original. That was how good a teacher Vangeli was. Some guys would not be convinced until I gave them a personal performance to prove that I was really playing the songs. The biggest tribute paid to me came from Vusi Mahlasela, one of SA's top guitarists, who came up to me after a performance at Moretele Park in Pretoria and complimented me on my playing. That was the kind of approbation I valued.

Basadi created a passion that was addictive—to the band and to the audience who loved to dance in a way that was new and joyous to me. For the first time I could see and hear and feel the power of music to bring people together. Growing up, we never listened to any black music in the house. When I joined Basadi a whole new world opened up to me.

The crowds at our shows were getting bigger too, and not only in the Johannesburg area. We were offered gigs some distance away which sometimes meant travelling for twenty-four hours simply for the pleasure of playing a one-hour show. It became a rigmarole to prepare all the equipment, organise the logistics of everyone's life to accommodate the trip, and then drive to some new venue in another province. The girls loved socialising for hours on end but all the down time generally left me quite lonely.

Sometimes we would score a great support gig for the likes of Hugh Masekela, for whom we often played and who always attracted a big crowd. However, Hugh had one stipulation whenever he added us to the line-up—he insisted Basadi always performed *after* his set. I like to think that either we were that good or our sound was too similar to his band that we might steal some of the impact of his show. He would want to play at midnight or later, whenever the mood suited him, which meant Basadi went on stage early on Sunday morning when everyone was well oiled.

Soon the band was playing bigger and bigger venues. We were tight, popular with the dance crowd, other bands admired us, and I always had my right-hand man, Vangeli, to underpin the whole sound. Surely nothing could go wrong, could it?

One day we were leaving Johannesburg to travel to some distant venue for a gig and the young Kombi driver, who had arrived late, was putting his foot to the floor to make up for lost time. On the highway outside Alberton the vehicle had a blow-out. One of the rear tyres had disintegrated and we veered off the highway into a field. Despite being thrown around like a rag doll I could see what was about to happen so I crouched into a ball on the floor. The driver completely lost control and we rolled over and over. Mabatho, Dineo, Zanele and Lily were all thrown through the windscreen and side windows before the van finally stopped rolling and ended up on its roof. Silence all around. When I got my wits back I managed to pull open the side door. I got out of the van and seriously thought the girls were goners. They were all lying on the veld and in bushes with no signs of life, looking like they had gone to heaven. But thank God they were only unconscious. Vangeli and the driver were still conscious so the three of us stumbled up to the road to wave down some help. No one would stop. I managed to call Dara, who arrived soon after with ambulances and paramedics. Dineo and Lily had serious pelvic breaks and spent a long time in hospital. Mabatho broke her fingers. Lily never fully recovered. I had serious pain in my chest; an X-ray revealed two fractured ribs. We had all been remarkably lucky as the van was a write-off. Somehow all our musical equipment escaped unscathed, but our injuries put the band out of commission for a long time.

Once the band members cleared their heads and thought about the reason for the accident, they decided that another all girl band had put a curse on us. It couldn't get any stranger. A decision was made that we should go to a traditional Sangoma, a spiritual healer, to cleanse us and give us protection against evil. The girls and Vangeli insisted that we *all* had to go or the Sangoma's powers would be ineffective. I was a bit nervous to say the least; I was more used to praying in church for Divine guidance and protection. Anyway, I went along with it; we were a band and we had to stick together. I agreed that I would take part in all the rituals short of drinking any concoctions because I knew my soccer players sometimes got violently ill from imbibing *muti* (liquid concoctions imbued with witchcraft). The potions were intended to cleanse the body and spirit inside and out, which usually meant a violently upset tummy (both ends) as all the evil was drawn out of you.

So we all traipsed off to downtown Johannesburg looking for a Sangoma to protect us from the evil intentions of our rival band. (That's a sentence I never thought I would write.) The Sangoma, located in a dingy shop displaying various animal parts in the window, handed us all kinds of bottles filled with strange liquids, not to drink but to rub over ourselves. The 'prescription', he explained, was to spread the gritty liquid all over our bodies before showering, and on the day of our next gig. I was sceptical but also happy to take part in the ritual as it seemed to both bond the band together in a unique way and somehow draw a line under the terrible accident. I don't suppose ZZ Top ever had to do it.

6

HEROES

Much later, by some miracle, Mabatho's manager got us a gig to play for former President Nelson Mandela at a highbrow state function. I had little to do with the manager, but for this gig I was forever grateful, a show which stands out as one of the proudest moments of my musical career. Who would have thought that little Fran from Driehoek, Germiston would one day play African jazz for Madiba, the most revered and loved man in the world. Pinch me!

Before we get to the gig I should explain a recurring problem that the band had to face, which often put our gigs in jeopardy. In common with Mervin, Vangeli had a taste for alcohol. Such was his need for a drink that he would often sell his keyboard for booze. Sometimes he would buy it back from the pawnbrokers, other times I had to borrow one to get us through a show. Somehow we always managed—just.

Shortly before the show of our lives, I had sold Vangeli my precious keyboard for a knockdown price—I knew he was struggling for cash and he could coax more music out of it than I ever could. The stars were aligning for a memorable night. Perhaps that concoction from the Sangoma had an effect after all...

This event should have been the highlight of my life so far, but turned into the most stressful gig ever. The event was held at Mahlamba Ndlopfu, the official presidential residence in Pretoria, a majestic old place built in the traditional Cape Dutch style. It was the most formal venue we had ever played. As usual I was first to arrive with all the drums, amps, PA system, and started to set up on a little stage at one end of a large room. Later the ladies wafted in struggling under the weight of a clarinet, flute or microphone. When the drums were set up and the cables connected, we did a sound check and were all ready to go, except for one omission. No Vangeli. Without him on keyboards we would be stumped. He left it to the last minute to make his entrance, just before we were due to kick off our set, but *without* the keyboard. We're on stage ready for the biggest gig of our lives with a keyboard player with no keys. The beautiful keyboard that I had practically paid him to take off my hands for the benefit of the band had been sold for drink. What was the point in him showing up without an instrument to play? More than a little worse for wear, he just stared at us with his big eyes not sure what to do next, probably believing that the mere fact that he had shown up at the president's place was success enough.

A thousand thoughts were racing through my head: could we get through the set without keys? Could we quickly source a keyboard from somewhere? Could I strangle Vangeli before the president walks in?

Madiba and his entourage were about to walk through the door so I had to find a solution fast. I had earlier spotted a dusty grand piano standing in the corner of the function room and, in desperation, decided we would have to use that. The whole band ran over to pull it closer to the stage and mic it up. In the kerfuffle that ensued one of the legs broke off. No panic, it's only the president's piano. We managed to hold up that end and drag the ungainly instrument across the room before propping it up on one of the PA speakers. As we looked around to see if any security had seen us wrecking the piano, Nelson Mandela stepped in. Everyone was standing and clapping as he made his entrance slowly and carefully, in true Madiba style. We picked up our instruments, Vangeli pulled the stool up to the piano and we were off, having snatched victory from the jaws of defeat.

After greeting various people and acknowledging the crowd, Madiba made his way to a table near the front of the house and took his seat among the dignitaries. I couldn't take my eyes off him, I was spellbound. Just to be in the same room as the great man was enough for me. But every time Madiba heard a song he knew—and I am sure he knew them all—he looked up and encouraged us with his trademark crinkly smile. I was hoping that he was thinking how amazing it was for a group of females—including this lone white woman—to be playing traditional African jazz standards so well. The song that really got his attention was the famous "Pata Pata", loosely translated as "Touch Touch", made famous by Miriam Makeba. By now the place was full of good vibes so he rose up out of his chair and proceeded to do his famous Madiba dance, fists clenched, hips swinging and arms rhythmically pumping in the air. He was not able to move his feet much so they remained planted on the floor, but the rhythm in his upper body more than made up for it. What more could a musician ask for? I felt that all my dreams had been fulfilled. They say you should never meet your heroes, but that unforgettable night was a wonderful exception to the rule.

I believed then that my brush with greatness would be a unique memory that would stay with me until my dying day. In fact, later that year I would meet the president once more, this time at closer quarters while wearing a Banyana Banyana cap, which I shall describe later.

Despite the occasional keyboard setback, Basadi continued to be invited to play more fancy shows. We were invited to play at a launch of a new British Airways route to Vic Falls. The whole band was flown up to the five-star Victoria Falls Hotel where we set up in the gardens and played while stunt planes flew under the railway bridge with trails of red, white and blue smoke. I wonder if the other girls in the band were thinking what I was thinking: *How the hell did we get here from those dingy rehearsal rooms in downtown Joburg?*

We didn't know it then but the British High Commissioner was at the show and, amazingly, invited Basadi Women of Jazz to represent Africa at a world music festival at the London Dome. The trip would be fully sponsored, flights included. Miracles do happen.

The London festival organisers wanted Basadi to be an all girl band (so did we, originally), but Vangeli was irreplaceable by this stage and we knew no one anywhere near as talented. We contemplated putting him in a wig but he wasn't keen on that idea. Having sacked our most recent vocalist for some negligence or other, we were also short of a singer, so we replaced her with Vicki who had sung in the Soweto Gospel Choir. We still had no regular drummer, so I asked the brilliant Annika Maswanganyi to join us. I returned to bass guitar.

We didn't tell the organisers that Vangeli was not a girl (Europeans couldn't tell from his name) and just accepted the opportunity to fly to London. My friend Leon also came along as sound engineer. Life was good.

On the day we arrived, for some reason the girls and Vangeli decided they had to go to the less than salubrious district of Brixton, south London, as if it was some kind of tourist destination. I had been there before and was not keen on a return visit. However, as our once-in-a-lifetime gig at the Dome was that evening, I thought it best we stick together and so caught the Tube with everybody else. While Brixton is on the same side of the River Thames as the Dome, it was a challenge to get there by people who were new to the Underground system.

Before splitting up in Brixton to see the 'sights' we all agreed to meet back at the Tube station at a set time to return to our accommodation together, get changed and head to the Dome. A couple of hours later everybody met at the agreed time, except Vangeli. We waited and waited. We couldn't leave without him, not only because he was central to the sound of the band, but also... what the hell was a cool dude from Soweto going to do alone in Brixton? Well, plenty actually. We split up to hit the local pubs to look for him. By sheer fluke we found him surrounded by some new-found friends in a local boozer having consumed countless bottles of beer. Luckily he could still stand. We brought him back with us and I didn't let him out of my sight until the gig... which went off without a hitch. The London crowd, sprinkled with plenty of tourists, seemed to appreciate some authentic African jazz on a grey day in Britain.

Another major gig we performed in later years was the send off for the South African team going to the 2012 London Olympics. For the event, held at the huge Vodaworld venue in Johannesburg, we had a sensational Sowetan singer called Emily who pitched up just before we went on to play to the packed 1000-seater room. But due to too much partying the night before—booze and funny cigarettes—she had completely lost her voice. It was the vocal equivalent of Vangeli showing up without his keyboard. The other girls in the band decided that I should replace her on vocals. Now, I could just about ad lib in the background to the African songs (more phonetic sounds than lyrics) but I didn't know the words. The only song I sang in the set was in English: "Stand by Me". Thank heavens that we had a brilliant sax player called Nola, who had to play her lungs out that night by covering the missing vocals with her solos.

The show must go on, so we had to focus on instrumentals to get through the night, stretching each song to twice their original length. People who knew our usual material were confused, including Dara who kept throwing her hands in the air as if the band had been hijacked. I decided then that I hated all lead singers—last to arrive at a gig, first to leave, they get all the attention, and if they don't show, the band is screwed.

But I wasn't rid of Emily just yet. We got signed to do a big gig for the Black Business Forum dinner, *the* black tie event of the year in the Johannesburg business world. It was held at the fancy Emperor's Palace, another 1000-seater venue. We were there (well, *I* was there) early to set up and soundcheck. The band, as usual, arrived looking for something to eat. This was their usual routine before every show, they had to eat before playing, which I always found curious because I was never hungry before a performance, rather the opposite because of nerves. Perhaps they had not eaten that day and they all needed sustenance to make it through the show. One thing was soon apparent to everyone: there was enough food and drink in the posh venue to feed the band for the rest of our careers.

So the place filled up, packed to the hilt with the great and the good in their jewels and sparkly outfits. We went down a storm. The guests were dancing non-stop and there were some terrific, happy vibes in the room. We had nailed it. The evening drew close to midnight, the time we were supposed to end the set, but the audience begged us to play longer and even offered more money, so of course we continued. As we were performing the last few songs of the night, people began drifting away as the venue emptied and we all felt the relief that followed another barnstorming show.

But Emily had other ideas. This was when I discovered she was another one who liked her alcohol a little too much. She was using a mic on a huge extension lead so she could mingle with the crowd while singing. Emily spotted the waiters clearing the tables, including full or nearly full bottles of wine which had been provided for the guests free of charge. She proceeded to climb off the stage, still singing, and waddle up to the empty tables to pinch the bottles before the waiters could clear them, then return to the bandstand and line them up on the edge of the stage. I was horrified, but I was playing drums and could do nothing to stop her. She continued with this embarrassing display until all the wine had been removed from the empty tables and we had about twenty bottles lined up on the stage. People obviously saw what she was doing and must have been appalled at the classless behaviour at such an upmarket event. Sensational voice or not, that's when we decided to part ways with Emily.

Memorable shows like playing at the presidential palace and the London Dome were what we all lived for. When great gigs happened I believed for that night that all the sacrifices were worth it. The feeling of kinship in the band, camaraderie with the audience, and the opportunity to get lost in music (yes, it really does happen in those rare moments) meant everything to me. But after some time I felt that, while I understood the hardships of living in a township, I was sacrificing more than others in the band. As I had the car, the trailer and a secure home environment (for which I was grateful), I had to shoulder the lion's share of responsibility. It was down to me to load and unload the trailer with all the unwieldy, heavy and expensive equipment for every show and make sure it was all secure. I was first to the soundcheck and last to leave after the gig. I also got tired of sneaking out from work to go to band practice. Inevitably the shows started to take their toll on me and the sheer physical effort expended for a ninety-minute set became tiresome. I still loved playing music at home but I had learned that the bigger the show the bigger the logistical headache. The moderate success of the band seemed to place us in a predicament—either we employed permanent roadies to help with the ever larger gigs or we lowered our expectations in terms of the venues we played.

I realised my heart was no longer in it. After a number of great, well-paying gigs, I had reached the end of the road with the band and announced that I was leaving. Vangeli also left; the two sisters, Mabatho and Dineo, continued as Basadi without me. It was a sad end to a great adventure, but if you're not feeling the joy anymore it is time to quit.

What of the man who taught me so much about music? Vangeli returned to his life in the shadows. The last I heard he had passed away in uncertain circumstances.

In later life, due to chronic arthritis, my index and middle fingers of my right hand (my guitar fretting hand) had to be fused. That saw the end of my guitar playing. The drumming also stopped because the osteoporosis was especially bad in my left elbow (probably from years of tennis in my youth). It calcified and any sudden movement became extremely painful.

Now that my playing days were over I had to replace those musical thrills by seeing as many top bands as possible. I would have to live my musical life vicariously. I was always an avid concert goer and never missed an opportunity to see live shows during the apartheid era when boycott-breaking artists such as Tina Turner, Cliff Richard, Suzi Quatro and Percy Sledge came to town. The rest of the Western world were probably appalled at these musicians breaking the artistic boycott, but we appreciated every tour from a big rock star.

Later, Elton John came to Johannesburg, unforgettable for his Donald Duck outfit, and silly Georgian wigs that were meant to disguise his thinning hair. Most memorable was his 1993 show on a hot summer night at Sun City's Valley of the Waves, which was emptied of water for the occasion. This was the infamous venue in Bophuthatswana, a previously so-called 'homeland' about 200 kms from Johannesburg that apartheid-era musicians played to sidestep the cultural boycott. Thousands were packed into the bottom of the empty pool, which made the usually hot and tropical atmosphere even sweatier. Elton played his grand piano from a rocky outcrop in all his splendour, bashing out all his well-loved songs. As he segued into a slow number, the light engineer switched off all the stage lights except for one spot that shone directly on his head. Of course, this being nighttime in North West province, swarms of moths and insects of various kinds were immediately attracted to the light and clustered around Elton's head. He tried valiantly to swipe them away with one hand while playing the keys with the other, but to no avail. The light engineer had not noticed this unfolding disaster but the audience could see the swarm of bugs growing rapidly—as was Elton's irritation.

Suddenly he jumped up from his piano and lost it completely. He started screaming like a banshee: 'Cant you f****** see the insects? What the f*** is wrong with you?' and many other expletives. The audience was shocked into silence and sympathy for him. The light engineer got the message and put on all the lights once more. Elton continued the show but the mood had been lost. He bashed his way through the rest of the set during which he refused to engage with the audience, then stormed off.

I saw him on one other occasion but this time he wised up and played in the National Botanical Gardens on a Saturday afternoon.

Other big names came out to South Africa as the country emerged out of the cultural boycott, although many were in the twilight of their careers and looking for a last lucrative tour: Roxette, Leo Sayer and Phil Collins come to mind. Other big names that trod a path to southern Africa were the Rolling Stones, Rod Stewart, Michael Jackson, U2, Bryan Adams and Black Eyed Peas.

Finally, when it came to stadium rock, for me there was one band that stood peerless: Queen. When I heard they were coming to perform a string of shows at Sun City in 1984 I nearly lost it. This was during the height of the boycott, but I didn't care about that—the band of my dreams was coming and I was determined to see them.

I was teaching at the time so had to bunk school on the day the tickets went on sale. I got there at 4 a.m.; the box office opened at 9 a.m. By lunchtime all 63,000 tickets were sold, two of them to me. I immediately booked my flight and a hotel. I was ready to rock and roll.

I couldn't wait for the concert to see the band in person so I bunked school again to be at Johannesburg Airport for their arrival. When they stepped into arrivals I was delirious. The airport was a madhouse. I was so close I could have reached out and touched Freddie if it wasn't for the hectic security. I can still remember his famous front teeth as he strode past me.

My sister Lynda, who had little interest in the band, managed to get a ticket for the first show. I did not like first nights, when bands often encounter problems with equipment or logistics that are worked out for later gigs. Big mistake. Lynda returned from the show on Saturday morning raving about how good the Friday night concert was. We prepared to head off to the airport to fly to our gig that night. Then someone switched on a radio. My world collapsed. The concert had been cancelled due to Freddie losing his voice... and the last show was full. I cried for a week.

Another band that came out to SA was Jethro Tull, a British heavy rock outfit. The ageing band toured South Africa in 1994 including a show at Carnival City in Boksburg. The packed theatre was filled with middle-aged fans, like us, who had resurrected their faded jeans, bandanas and T-shirts that were now stretching over bulging waistlines.

Before the show kicked off a compere came on stage and said that we were not allowed to shout or scream or applaud while the band was playing. No misbehaving, jumping around and dancing and screaming? What were all the middle-aged rockers supposed to do now? Sit politely with folded arms?

Their songs were exceptionally intricate so I guess they had to have quiet to hear each other. But the band were wooden. The only one who seemed to be able to move at all was the flautist and singer Ian Anderson. After each song the compere would pop up and indicate that we could now applaud. Now *that* was extraordinary for a rock gig.

The big moment arrived when they launched into their hit song "Locomotive Breath". Because we were not allowed to make a noise we all sat noiselessly singing away in our heads and playing imaginary instruments with our fingers. The flute then broke into the much-loved lead solo, which should have been followed by the renowned guitar solo... but where was the guitarist? He had gone AWOL. The rest of the band carried on valiantly, trying to cover up this vital section of the song. As the band approached the end of the track the guitarist re-appeared but he had long missed his cue. We all wondered what had happened. After the final chord the singer had the decency to explain: 'Sorry about that, everyone, but at our age when you gotta go you gotta go!'

In 2017 Dara and I decided to visit London for a short break. As we were sorting out the booking I saw that Adele was going to perform four shows around that time at the newly rebuilt Wembley Stadium. I begged the travel agent to change the dates and get us tickets. Success. We didn't even think about the price. Frankly, I would have paid anything.

I will never forget that wonderful night at Wembley. I was in my element. This time we were lucky to have picked the second show because she cancelled her last two concerts after losing her voice. I suppose it was some justice after missing Freddie and the boys.

I didn't only see international superstars. A local favourite and role model of mine was Johnny Clegg—musician, dancer, anthropologist and human rights activist. I tried not to miss his live shows if at all possible. When he was a youngster of seventeen he teamed up with Zulu musician Sipho Mchunu, who taught him to speak the language and play the traditional maskandi guitar. Boy, could he do the Zulu tribal dances! Clegg formed Juluka in the seventies and became an anti-apartheid activist, for which he was arrested many times. He wrote a song for the imprisoned Nelson Mandela, called "Asimbonanga" (translation, "We have not seen him"). After his release, during one memorable concert, Mandela came on stage while Clegg was singing his song.

Johnny Clegg passed away in 2019 and will always be remembered as much for trying to bridge the racial divide in South Africa as for his powerful music.

7

WIND IN MY HAIR

My commitments to music, football and rowing took plenty of my free time during the 1980s and 90s, but there was one interest that fired me up like no other. Despite my meagre income from teaching I always made sure I had enough left over to indulge my other great passion: bikes. They say you don't understand why a dog puts its head out of a car window until you ride a motorbike. Well, it was true for me.

From the Yamaha 125cc I moved up a few rungs on the two-wheeled ladder when I graduated to my first serious bike, a black Honda K1, a powerful and beautiful 750cc beast that I bought from my brother-in-law Billy. I spent hours polishing the paintwork and buffing up the chrome. It came with the noisiest exhaust system around because he had taken out the silencer so that pedestrians and other road users could hear the bike coming from a mile away. 'Noise saves lives,' he would say gleefully. *And send the neighbours into meltdown*, I would think.

When you buy your first big bike, there is one thing you want to do more than anything: join a gang and show it off. So I joined the Phantom Riders and ventured out on my first bike gathering—the 1990 Rhino Rally in Estcourt, KwaZulu-Natal, a wild and promiscuous event still spoken about by bikers as the best ever rally. Many did not even make it to the rally as bike accidents en route were commonplace. I made it in one piece, but I had low rider handlebars on the Honda and halfway down to Estcourt my neck seized up from holding my head at such an unnatural angle. I later changed to upright bars.

The campsite was located in a huge pleasure resort park and I knew right away that I had arrived somewhere special. Other biker gangs had equally fearsome names such as Hell's Angels, Devil's Advocates, Sons of Satan. It was a huge honour to earn your gang 'colours' (official gang acceptance in the form of a stitch-on badge), which proved that you now belonged to the 'family'. It wasn't easy to prove that you fitted in. Some gangs made new recruits perform initiation rituals. Prospective Phantom Rider recruits had to wait a year to earn colours during which time they had to prove they could *avoid* drunkenness and fighting. Another visible sign of devotion to the cause was to add pins or badges to your jacket that proved attendance at various rallies such as the Buffalo, the Impala, etc. The more memorabilia you had, the more revered you were.

Back to the Rhino rally—5,000 bikers and 'chicks' (girls riding pillion) assembled in quiet Estcourt for a weekend of debauchery and drunken rowdiness. Once you parked up your bike, the main priority was to drink as much of as many different types of alcohol as possible. For the guys, having a chick on the back of the bike was essential, preferably one dressed as skimpily as possible. The biggest applause was always for the topless pillion girls. The bigger the boobs the louder the appreciation. It was amazing how apparently 'normal', respectable people—doctors, lawyers, teachers—joined the rally and turned from respectable Dr Jeckyls into speed freak Mr Hydes. As soon as they donned the leather jacket, Levis, boots and sleeveless denim waistcoat emblazoned with the gang logo on the back, they transformed into crazy drunken lunatics.

The campsite had a long smooth strip in the middle used by bikers to 'dice' or race each other. At the end of the seventy-five-metre strip was a six-metre drop into a stream. Both drunk bikers and sober ones raced each other to the end of the strip, neither wanting to be the first to brake. By the end of the weekend the stream was full of wrecked machinery. Thousands of rands worth of beautiful bikes down the drain—or rather down the river. Some bikers didn't bother to use the strip but rather raced around the park where they crashed into each other anyway. Many of those not racing spent much of their time revving their bike's engine for the noise and the sheer pleasure of seeing the rev counter hit the red line.

There was also a ramp, which had probably been used for water skiing at one point, that bikers would ride up to get lift-off, often smashing up the bikes on landing.

Between the bike races, insane revving, shouting and catcalls, there was never a moment when music wasn't being blasted out of overdriven speakers. Some crazy guy had been hired to be the DJ but the only tape he seemed to have brought was Pink Floyd's *The Wall*. He was obsessed with that record. I still sometimes wake up singing "Another Brick in the Wall".

There was rarely any belligerence between the gangs because each was afraid that if you picked a fight with someone, the rest of their gang would descend, and you were never sure if your gang was larger than theirs.

Chatting up another gang's chicks was also a big no-no and could result in a serious beating. The first-aid tent was permanently full with injured, beaten-up or just plain paralytic bikers and their chicks.

Some bikers brought a spare rear tyre so they could ruin one in a burn-out while being cheered on by the drunken crowd that soon disappeared in a smokescreen of scorching rubber until the tyre eventually burst. While that was going on, inside a big tent some of the male bikers were dancing on top of the rubbish bins with naked lower halves. That sight taught me never to judge a book by its cover.

Amongst this chaotic scene there was a gang called the Riders for the Son, a Christian group who would give out free coffee from their stand, probably to try to sober up the bikers and preach against the error of their ways. They would hold church services on the Sunday for those who were still conscious. I found it hard to understand why they would want to come and witness such moral turpitude. They probably hoped they could save a few lost souls, and perhaps they did.

This may all sound rather depraved, but to little old Fran, my dream of becoming a bad-ass biker girl had finally been realised. Despite the heavy drinking and regularly dicing with death on two wheels, I decided the Phantom Riders were not hardcore enough for me. I imagined riding with the Hell's Angels, although they would never allow women riders. Nevertheless we had some girls in our gang who were as fierce as any Hell's Angel, such as my amazing friend Bernie (the one who shot a hole in the roof of the hotel and not to be confused with my guitarist). A short girl, Bernie could skilfully handle a big Kawasaki 1100cc and pop wheelies better than anyone I ever met. Sitting astride the bike, her tiptoes hardly touched the ground and she would often drop it at walking speed as it was so heavy to wheel around. She didn't care. She was a veteran of a number of serious bike accidents but she was never put off. After a few drinks she would challenge bikers twice her size with the baddest bikes either to a race or to a fight, whichever they preferred. Believe it or not this seemingly out of control bundle of energy had once been a Johannesburg traffic cop. She must have been fearsome. She then reduced the driving force under her to one horsepower when she moved on to the mounted police. Unfortunately she was kicked by a horse and had to retire from the force.

Bikers and chicks usually slept in small two-person tents. Different gangs camped in designated areas of the campsite, the Phantom Riders taking space at the bottom of a hill. Some also spent the night in the big main tent, but sleep was not an activity indulged in much on rallies. Nobody came to catch up on their beauty sleep. As soon as one guy passed out drunk, another would wake up, take his keys and start revving his bike mercilessly.

And then it would rain. Our cheap tents were hardly waterproof so everyone was soon covered in mud. And the only thing that would keep us going on this weekend binge? An egg and bacon roll at breakfast, just enough to line the tummy for the day's hard drinking ahead.

The Saturday night was always the big event in the main tent and featured a live band. We were all subjected to the Miss Rhino competition (topless chicks) and the Mr Big Boep competition (biggest beer belly), which encouraged much raucous behaviour and drunken dancing until the early hours.

On the Sunday morning, when the campsite looked like the aftermath of a pitched battle, local families from Estcourt came down to catch a glimpse of the dissolute biker community. What a shock awaited them. The sunrise saw a slew of catatonic bodies lying in ungraceful poses around the campsite or zombie-like people searching for their tents. There were piles of crashed bikes everywhere, hungover bikers staggering around like the walking wounded and scantily clad chicks wondering where the hell they were. Then two skinny guys, already drunk, wandered past with their willies tied together with string, and boy they had willies—fourteen inches or more. The locals are probably still talking about them.

The sun was up, I had a long ride home, and I had to teach a class of teenagers at school the following morning, so it was time for me to leave. As I mentioned, we had pitched our camp at the bottom of a short hill so I had to ride up the steep incline to get out of the camp. My front brake was kaput so I had to rely solely on the rear brake. But to climb up the incline I had to stand up on the pegs and was unable to reach the rear brake with my right foot. I braced myself, opened the throttle and headed for the top of the hill. As I reached the summit, effectively with no brakes, I rode straight through a pitched tent with an unsuspecting couple sleeping inside. They were not impressed and the man came out screaming blue murder. I skidded off.

I attended a number of rallies over the years but none compared with the Rhino for sheer wanton depravity. After each one, the organiser Simon Fourie swore blind he would never do another because of all the trouble. But he always came back the following year, as did I.

Believe it or not the rally I have described was one of the better organised. At another rally, in Cullinan, my brother-in-law Billy booked what he believed was suitable accommodation off-site. The 'accommodation' turned out to be a run-down boarding school or hostel of some kind with one communal shower and toilet for twelve biker guys and chicks. That meant sagging ancient spring beds and thin, wiry mattresses. Even the sleeping bags we had luckily packed did not keep out the freezing cold or the noise from the railway line on which we were inconveniently located.

Now that I was becoming a hardened biker, I started an all girl biking gang with my hotheaded friend Bernie. We placed an ad in the paper to which about a dozen girls replied, who were all keen to join. We adopted the name Libra for some long forgotten reason. One of the girls was another crazy girl biker who I will never forget called Maxine, a ladylike Jewish girl who had no right to be let loose on a powerful bike. She was absolutely useless at riding her big 650cc, but was determined and fearless so she fitted into the Libra gang perfectly. She was forever misjudging her cornering and going off the road onto grass verges or hitting barrels and barriers. But she would not be deterred. On one particular ride I was leading the pack at the required 120 kph. Out of the blue I saw Maxine screaming past me on the wrong side of the road. I gave chase and waved her down. When she finally realised it was me, she said she didn't recognise anyone she was riding with and had thought we were some other group so was trying to catch up to her own gang.

However, it was not all gang camaraderie and getting into biking scrapes. Sometimes four wheels were as dangerous as two. There were two girls in the gang, my ex Virginia (the keyboard player from Kamikazi) and Carla, who were in a relationship. Carla, a beautiful Portuguese girl, was killed in a car crash while travelling back from Durban with Virginia. I helped Virginia with her long recovery from serious injuries, including breaking her jaw.

Later that year she gave birth to a girl who she named Carla in honour of her friend. She did not know she was pregnant until she was six months gone because she had lost so much weight due to her mouth being wired up and only able to drink liquids.

I stepped in to help raise the baby girl. Later Dara was also involved in her upbringing. I loved Carla from the word go. I took her in to my home and she became a vital part of my life. On one occasion, when she was still a toddler, the rowing team was desperate to train for the Wemmer Pan Championships, so I wrapped her in a lifejacket, perched her on the bow of the boat and went out for the practice. The rowing club chairman came past in his speedboat to check on the crews but was not impressed by my waterborne childcare arrangements and made us return to shore.

The child grew into a fine woman who subsequently had two boys of her own, to whom I have always followed the 'grannies guidebook' to a T, spoiling them rotten whenever I can. To this day she feels like my own child.

Back in the world of biking, my next motorcycle reflected a more sedate riding experience. I traded in the Honda black beast for a pale blue Yamaha 1100cc cruiser, complete with leather tassels on the handlebars. It was an altogether more relaxed low rider with plenty of chrome that suited me well and meant I could happily sit on it with both feet firmly planted on the ground. Dara insisted the bike had to have a backrest on the pillion seat from which she could sit in comfort and enjoy the scenery. Having left the girl gangs behind, our riding now consisted of breakfast runs to Hartebeespoort Dam where thousands of bikes congregated on Sundays.

My biking days finally came to an end after I had two knee replacements and tearfully had to sell the bike.

8

HELLO WORLD

It may seem barely credible now but while I was immersing myself in the slightly unhinged world of biking, I was still devoted to the disciplines of high level sport, i.e., football. By the mid-80s my playing days were coming to an end and it was taking all my time and dedication to run the Eastern Transvaal Women's League with no sponsorship and no pay. Despite those shortcomings I threw myself into it heart and soul. I knew there was a future for women's football in South Africa so unless I got off my behind and did something about it there was no use complaining.

In 1987 I received my ten-year provincial representation badge. The following year I was approached by Joseph Mkhonza (known as 'Skesh'), a former Kaizer Chiefs player who ran a women's team in the Kwa-Thema township and wanted to join our Sunday league. This was an exciting development. Contravening clear guidance against the immoral mixing of the races, I happily agreed. Although we were still living under the appalling apartheid laws, which insisted on different leagues for different races, no one seemed to worry about two female teams of various races running around on a Sunday, so we just got on with it. Such a modest episode can now be seen as a breakthrough for multiracial football in South Africa, and about time too. At the time, white men were regularly arrested if they played in or against black or coloured teams, and vice versa. It was a sporting example of how ridiculous apartheid was, and how forward-thinking us women were in breaking down barriers.

This extraordinary state of affairs may require some explanation. Growing up in a largely white environment, my friends and I were constantly warned of the *swart gevaar*, the black danger. The population was indoctrinated because all aspects of the media were controlled by the white government. SABC radio news and state-run newspapers, essentially mouthpieces for the ruling National Party, stoked the divisions of racism with its obedient support for the apartheid system. It got no better when South Africa introduced television in 1976. It just meant that now we were shown closely edited news footage that stoked that same racism. We were reminded at every turn that the African National Congress were the most terrible communists who had only one aim: to overrun the white minority—that is if they didn't murder us in our beds first. We saw what the government wanted us to see; we read what they wanted us to read; we spoke to whom they wanted us to speak. When you're told something so relentlessly over so many years, you end up believing it because you reason that there must be no alternative.

The one aspect of my life that seemed to contradict the nationalist line was the fact that my family were Catholics, and black people were allowed to worship in our church. The sacraments were the same for everybody: black churchgoers sat on the same pews, prayed the same prayers, sang the same hymns and took the same Holy Communion. Presumably they went to the same heaven. They certainly didn't look like communists planning to overthrow the government.

Also, my convent school had always admitted black pupils from Zimbabwe (Rhodesia, as was) and other African countries, so, a young Fran often asked herself, what was so terrible about black people? For years we were warned that the country was on the verge of a civil war, and that whites had to protect themselves from the inevitable insurgency. But when, in 1989, it became clear that Mandela would be released from prison, paradoxically the mood in the white neighbourhoods softened. For years the leader of the ANC was demonised as the spawn of the devil but as his release approached, the word on the street was that, far from calling for insurrection, he could be the man to save the country.

The excitement of his release on 11 February 1990, the subsequent end of apartheid, and the first democratic elections in April 1994, fuelled a spirit in the country in which many people believed anything was possible. Including me. South Africa would no longer be a pariah in the community of nations, no longer a by-word for racism (even though we still have much work to do on that front), and all the institutions that were suspended could now take their place alongside their counterparts around the world.

However, until we had a peaceful transfer of power, the calm was fragile. It might take just one moment of lunacy from a hothead to upset the new order. That moment seemed to come in April 1993 when an anti-communist radical shot and killed Chris Hani, the leader of the South African Communist Party and chief of staff of *uMkhonto we Sizwe*, the armed wing of the ANC. On the day of his funeral I was standing on the corner of President Street in Germiston when busloads of black mourners drove past on the way to the memorial. The fragile mood was a mixture of sadness and anger. I was scared. That day seemed to me to be a tipping point, which luckily tipped towards peace, but could so easily have ignited the country into flames.

Despite the murder of his friend and cadre, Mandela appealed for calm and managed to defuse the volatile atmosphere in the country. I knew then that he was the only man who could create a new country worth living in, and who had no interest in revenge or making the whites 'pay' for apartheid and his years of incarceration. I was so heartened by Mandela's dignified bearing, his presence on the world stage and his ability to find common ground rather than deepen divisions, that I am proud to say I voted for the ANC in the first democratic elections in 1994. The modern ANC, leaving a trail of corruption wherever they go, is a very different beast to those heady days when Madiba was the conscience of the world. Then we lived on belief; now we live on hope.

What was so impressive about Mandela was his preaching a gospel of forgiveness. It helped undermine the influence of the trigger-happy members of the ANC, calmed the fears of the right-wing whites, and encouraged the world to see that South Africa was worthy of returning to the global village. The country should be eternally grateful to him for that. Heaven knows the mess we may have been in if he had been a hothead.

As a consequence of these major political changes, SAFA was constituted in 1991 and admitted to FIFA the following year. It promised exciting times for people like me who were keen to see the game grow.

With changes in football moving on apace I needed to make a decision about whether to stay in the sport in a thankless administrative capacity or put the sport behind me. But there was a third option I had not considered: become a coach. Even though there were no professional female coaches in South Africa at the time, and no role models to emulate, I decided to try my hand. I knew I would be on my own and accepted that it would be difficult, but even I had no idea what almighty battles lay ahead.

However, despite a distinct lack of support from the male dominated game, my timing was quite fortuitous. I heard that FIFA was going to hold its first ever Futuro coaching course in South Africa at Esselen Park, Kempton. First come first served, said the organisers. I was there at 7 a.m., the first in the queue to register.

When the organisers showed up, I was told to wait. I waited. And waited. Men started pitching up and were immediately registered and sent off to get their coaching kit. In spite of my gentle reminders, once more I was told to wait. Perhaps the organisers were hoping that all the places would be taken before they could tell me 'better luck next time'.

As the course filled up I began to worry that I may miss this golden opportunity. The clock ticked past lunchtime. No one wanted to help me. I was reduced to tears. Eventually Dara, who had dropped me off and planned to stay until I had registered, lost it completely. When the first SAFA CEO, Solomon 'Stix' Morewa, and the president, Molefi Olifant, arrived to open the event, she verbally attacked them and told them how I had been first in the queue but had been ignored. They gave in in the face of two determined women and, somewhat reluctantly, told the organisers, Peruvian ex-pro Augusto Palacios and Derek Blanckensee (later to become the Premier Soccer League's general manager), to register me and provide me with kit. I resented their begrudging acceptance of a woman on the course, but at least I was in, and had to put the episode down to just another niggling struggle for women in football.

Then the outlook turned still brighter. While Dara was hanging around offering me moral support, she started talking to some doctors she knew from her days as a nursing sister. They said they were there for the FIFA medical course, which was running concurrently. One of them suggested she join them. She did, and got herself registered. We both got FIFA certificates.

I started following world football closely from the inaugural 1991 FIFA Women's World Cup in China (sixty-one years after the men's competition began). It makes you wonder what took them so long. I was glued to the TV coverage from China—the stats, the punters, the crowds—and astounded by the form of the USA girls who were pure class, especially Golden Shoe winner Michelle Akers-Stahl. My only regret was not being there.

Seeing the World Cup matches on TV was one thing; experiencing them in the flesh would be quite another. The day the USA captain April Heinrichs lifted the trophy I decided I was going to the next World Cup in Sweden, no matter what. I was still teaching at that time so earned a relative pittance, but I was determined to do whatever it took to pay for the flight. I even gave guitar lessons to make a bit extra. I scrimped and saved for the next four years.

Meanwhile I was doing my level best to get South African women's football onto a better footing. It was still in its infancy so we had a long way to go to meet the standards of our esteemed contemporaries. But at some point we had to get out of our own way. The USA team may have benefited from the correct training, nutrition, support, encouragement, ambition, and all the things we lacked, but they were still only eleven women just like my team. Was it madness to dream that one day the South

African women's senior team could walk out into a World Cup stadium?

Every success has to start somewhere. And for this I am grateful for the dedication of a few hardy souls who could see the big picture and kept going for little or no reward. In this category I would place my life partner Dara who was the unpaid national team manager during the early 1990s at a time when we struggled to get even the most basic equipment. The players had to make do with only one kit, a tracksuit and two T-shirts each—and that was thanks to Emy Casaletti who pulled some strings at sportswear firm Kappa. After each training camp Dara would meticulously collect every item, bring it home, wash it and pack it away ready for the next camp. The kit lasted five years and we never lost a thing. When she left the job to focus on her full-time occupation, the kit disappeared after the first camp.

Caring for the kit was the least of her responsibilities. In 1995 Dara was sent with the team to Angola, which had recently come out of a tumultuous civil war. At that time we had no technical support staff; it was just the coach, Sandile Bali, Reuben Magoshoa as head of delegation (HOD), and team manager Dara Carroll. She had to take up the slack in the system, which meant dealing with any and all eventualities, including acting as the team seamstress, and was forever sewing on names and numbers or covering up forbidden branding on team jerseys. As a nurse she was also called upon to act as medic and psychologist. No wonder she was known to the team as Mama Dara.

On one trip to Zambia the goalkeeper got seriously ill and Dara had to take her by army vehicle to an overcrowded hospital where patients were sleeping on the floor or lying under occupied beds waiting their turn for treatment. She was often sent into remote areas of Nigeria without a penny of SAFA funds, and resorted to waving her own credit card to demand treatment, then later fight to get the money reimbursed. I was always left feeling guilty when she later retold these tales because I had pushed her to take on the role of manager. Stuck in some shabby African town with no money, I'm sure she cursed me at times.

I still find it shocking that SAFA would treat one of their representatives so indifferently. Now that women's football in South Africa is on a more secure footing, perhaps there should be some financial acknowledgement for all the years when staff and players performed for no monetary reward.

Generally speaking, African teams were lagging behind the herd—with one exception: the Super Falcons. Back in 1991 Nigeria was the only African team at the first women's World Cup in China, which gave them an early opportunity to judge themselves against world class competition. Even though the Super Falcons would subsequently attend almost every women's World Cup, they rarely reached the final stages because they, in common with most African nations, did not compete enough, and were rarely match fit. African squads would often assemble specially for the Confederation of African Football (CAF) competition, held every second year; then after the tournament the team would pack it in as there were no organised leagues worth the effort to keep fit and trained enough to entertain fans. European national teams played all year round, so we were always on the back foot. We needed the newly incorporated South African Football Association to lead from the front.

SAFA was formed by combining the different organisations that had previously been run by race group —coloured, Indian, white, etc. Meanwhile, SAWFA, the women's equivalent association, was already well-established, well-organised, independent and solvent (and, unofficially, racially colour-blind).

Even though SAFA was principally concerned with men's football, we had to join the new organisation to be recognised by FIFA, the world body. We were told to formally request affiliation at a meeting in Joburg in 1993. The SAFA board had never met us but I was sure they would expect a group of white women and men to arrive for affiliation. But our SAWFA committee had long been multiracial and was lucky to include the likes of Mary-Jane Sokela, Thembi Khumalo and Gloria Sibande. We also had a coloured man from Western Cape in the mix, Lionel Williams.

So we walked in to this meeting and the SAFA board—all men—were gobsmacked to see our mixed, mostly female SAWFA committee that represented women's football. Once they got over the shock they said that they would accept us, but only as an *associate* member. Thanks for having us, guys.

Now that South Africa was recognised by FIFA, in 1993 ex-Southampton FC pro Terry Paine was taken on as coach and a national women's team was selected, which included a sprinkling of players from the club side Soweto Ladies, a team that will return to my story later. Our first FIFA-approved international was against Zimbabwe, away. We won. We then played our first home international against Swaziland on 30 May that year. We won 14–0. It was a great welcome back into world football, and remained our biggest ever win until our defeat of Comoro Islands 17–0 in 2019.

The following year by chance I heard of an upcoming CAF instructor's course. It would be led by the legendary Ghanaian coach Charles Gyamfi, the first African to play professionally in Germany and winner (as coach) of three African Cup of Nations titles with the national team, the Black Stars. I simply *had* to attend the course. With much begging and scraping once more to the SAFA officials, I got on the course with all the leading coaches and big-name former professionals. As usual I was the only woman. Looking back, this proved to be the second, life changing step on my road towards a professional career in football.

Around this time I also met the successful Kaizer Chiefs coach Ted Dumitru, a Romanian by birth who had lived in South Africa for many years. His approach to the game was way ahead of our conventional style, and he used interesting concepts such as a form of systematic training known as periodization, a new idea to us. At that time there were few avenues for coaches to learn, so attendees would travel from Soweto, Vaal and Pretoria to be at the Johannesburg venue on a Monday night. Attendees were mainly black with some white and coloured coaches, all eager to learn from a proven leader. We hung on his every word. Inspiring days. Ted then moved the course to Esselen Park and the numbers grew (but still no other women joined). Other coaches who attended his courses, such as Sam Mbatha (most recently the head of youth development at Mamelodi Sundowns) and Farouk Khan (director of coaching at Stars of Africa football academy), went on to achieve big things.

Ted later became SAFA technical director. He passed away in 2016 but is regarded as a South African coaching legend whose approach to the game is still revered.

By the end of the course I could see a future for me in football. I was finally being taken seriously as a coach and the standard of play at under-17, under-19 and senior age groups was improving. The women's association was gaining credibility and the future looked bright for women's football—that was until the 1994 inter-provincial tournament in Eastern Transvaal.

As SAWFA gained strength through the increased number of affiliated teams, a streamlined organisation, and an improvement in our public profile, a group of five men emerged on the scene, mainly from Soweto, some from Eastern Transvaal, who decided that *they* wanted to run women's football because they had recently 'adopted' some black teams, the most prominent of which was Soweto Ladies. This cabal protested to SAFA that our organisation was not representative across the colour line, and that we were racist, which was a calumny. Anyone with eyes in their head could see the make-up of our teams and board members as proof that we were clearly not racist. I was not only more than a little peeved that this group wanted to take over all the good work we had done, I also questioned their motives. Why would a bunch of middle-aged men want to take control of a sport that attracted a never-ending stream of fit, young females? You work it out.

Unfortunately SAFA, led by Molefi Olifant and Stix Morewa, entertained their grievances. That's when the problems started. The new faction of men mistakenly believed there was money in women's football, which was why they contrived a takeover—but alas there was none.

So, it's 1994, and this group of insurgents arrive at the inter-provincial tournament in Eastern Transvaal with their *own* mainly black team, purporting to represent Southern Transvaal. They took to the field during a game featuring the *legitimate* Southern Transvaal (and also mainly black) team and staged a sit-in. Now there were twenty-two players from the Southern Transvaal facing eleven from Western Cape. The infiltrators had also bussed down their own supporters, so the situation quickly became volatile and the police were called to calm the situation. I was left scratching my head at how easy it was to create bedlam over something so petty, and which seemed to perfectly reflect the political volatility in the country at that time. Never ones to exercise a softly softly approach, the police arrived in Casspir armoured vehicles and chased the intruding team and their followers away.

The incident made all the newspapers and certainly created a splash for women's football.

Despite winning a moral victory on the day, the problem of who should organise and run women's football had not been resolved. SAFA would have to make a judgment. To this end a hastily created 'crisis committee' of mainly men was convened in Gauteng. Meanwhile, female players from the teams they controlled were coerced against registering with SAWFA or joining established teams. Astonishingly SAFA supported *them* rather than their own legitimate affiliate, SAWFA.

Then it got personal. Many on the opposing side made it clear that they saw me as the problem because I had no qualms complaining to anyone who would listen about the unjust situation. Consequently I drew a lot of fire from our opponents, literally in some cases. The crisis became more serious for me when I was subject to regular silent phone calls and threatened with death on more than one occasion. One day someone cruised slowly down the road and shot at my house. Then my vice president, Thembi Khumalo, was threatened that she and her children would be harmed and her house burnt down if SAWFA did not relinquish control of women's football.

I had to take stock of the situation. Was this really happening, or was I just imagining the threats? Late the following evening I got a call from one of the men I suspected of waging the campaign of terror. He complained that someone closely associated with the crisis committee was now shooting at *him*. He must have had a falling out after some internal disagreement, and now he was turning to me for help. The situation couldn't get more ludicrous. We were clearly up against people who had connections in the seedy end of town, but all we could do was keep our heads down and hope reason would prevail. I laid a charge at the police station and reported the situation to SAFA. Even though nothing came of it, events had clearly come to a head. Women's football couldn't continue this way.

The crisis committee then came up with make-believe provincial structures (that nobody had ever heard of), a move that was intended to outweigh our influence. However, the main footballing provinces were already affiliated to SAWFA. We therefore asked the committee to produce some kind of evidence that would prove the existence of these organisations, such as names of teams, officials, registered players, etc. Despite my regular protestations to SAFA and the crisis committee, they would not (or perhaps could not) present any membership documents.

SAFA then appointed six members from SAWFA and six from the crisis committee to meet and work out the issues. Mediators were appointed, which included national sports commission member Kedi Tshoma and SAFA board member Reuben Mogoshoa. But the talks went nowhere and the other side wasted valuable time 'caucusing', a word I had never heard used in this context, but which was becoming, it seemed to me, a convoluted method of getting their own way. We would have endless fruitless meetings to discuss something with the crisis committee and then they would have to go out and caucus. This invariably took hours. We should never have been subjected to this.

Meanwhile, there was a sinister backdrop to all the shenanigans at the meetings. There were a number of claims of sexual harassment against one of the men. As I had feared, this group wanted their hands on more than just the purse strings. With my assistance, two of the Soweto Ladies players lodged a police case against the man—which was the last we heard about it. It was a case of he said–she said, and without clear evidence, the police dropped the investigation (if there ever was one).

I was not satisfied with the response to the situation, so I called up the City Press who ran the story of the allegations on their front page, which ruffled a few feathers in the SAFA offices. So much so that I was hauled in for a showdown with the top brass who told me to withdraw my support for the abused women because I was ruining the man's reputation. They were more annoyed that one of their own was attracting negative headlines, and showing no compassion for the women who had been mistreated. That was typical of the attitude I was up against time and again.

There was another occasion in the mid-90s, at a tournament held in Cape Town, where a number of teams arrived and I realised I had another problem. In the hotel I saw two male SAFA officials calling young players down to reception from their rooms and seemingly trading them with other officials. I was horrified.

Administrators have a duty of care to players—male and female—so I was determined to voice my objections and make the necessary changes. Consequently I fought to get a SAFA ruling passed that stipulated one of the match officials at women's games had to be a woman. To this day that ruling stands.

I learned another hard lesson at an Eastern Transvaal tournament around the same time. The Mpumalanga provincial team arrived with their coach, a man called Little Joe. Their team manager was a woman. During the tournament I came upon a loud argument between the coach and the manager. On investigation I discovered that she, the manager, was Little Joe's wife. He had been fraternising with the girls in the team and she was now performing as only a scorned wife can.

This proved to me that male coaches and administrators had too much control over young players. It was too easy for players who were desperate to play to fall prey to coaches who had the power to either put them in the starting eleven or drop them. The first country to make headlines about this in Southern Africa was Swaziland (now Eswatini) when players accused the coach of unacceptable behaviour. The problem persists in many countries around the world. You want to make the team? Then sleep with the coach.

This is not a uniquely African problem. In 2019 the president of the Afghan Football Federation, Keramuudin Karim, was banned for life when female players exposed his sexual, physical and emotional abuse. FIFA also banned Yves Jean-Bart, the president of the Haiti Football Federation, from all football-related activities and fined him 1 million Swiss francs after its ethics committee found him guilty of having sexually harassed and abused female players, including minors.

Incidents like these made me realise that I had to do what I could to empower women, especially the majority black women, to be strong and take the lead in the sport. Consequently later in life I embarked upon a programme to develop female coaches and administrators, and made it a priority to put structures and programmes in place that swung the balance of power towards women in the game. There is still a long way to go to achieve parity but I believe I have left a lasting legacy in this regard.

Back to my struggle with the so-called crisis committee. I decided to look for allies outside SAFA. I started to write letters, lots of them; in fact it turned into a campaign. Almost daily (no exaggeration) I wrote to the then Minister of Sport Steve Tshwete and Director General of Sport Mthobi Tyamzashe. I complained about how Olifant and Morewa were supporting an outside group that should have been told to affiliate to the officially recognised women's football body, SAWFA. (Years later Mthobi said that he had received more letters from me in one year than all his other mail put together.) Frustrated and at my wits' end, I also started writing letters to President Nelson Mandela in the hope that he would intervene in some way to resolve the situation. His secretary replied that he was unavailable, but at least I had registered my predicament with his office.

I was fed up with SAFA's dismissive attitude to the women's game and all that we had achieved, and insulted by their archaic, sexist attitudes. On one occasion I attended a function and Morewa and Olifant were there with Steve Tshwete. Stix Morewa said to me, 'Go and give Steve Tshwete a kiss and he will help you!' This was typical of his facetious attitude to me. Whenever the SAFA National Executive Committee (NEC) held meetings, there would be a bevy of beautiful ladies waiting in reception for some post-meeting fun. Solly P was in charge of them—and don't any outsider dare chat up their girls.

After months of letter writing (and I do mean letters, no email then), in 1995 Steve Tshwete put a commission in place to hear our grievances, which I like to think came about because of my letters to President Mandela. Judge Pickard was appointed to head the commission of investigation and hear us out.

Despite football's dirty laundry being aired in public, the threats against SAWFA committee members continued unabated. Now it was the turn of my other vice-president, Mary-Jane Sokela, to be threatened. Judge Pickard heard about the threats and instructed her to keep her whereabouts a secret and to change her flights from Durban to the commission at short notice. Top sports journalist Thomas Kwenaite was also threatened for writing about the allegations in glorious detail. The situation quickly became volatile, so much so that on the second day of the investigation a metal detector was installed to check everybody for weapons as they entered the downtown office building where the commission was being held.

After much toing and froing for weeks on end, Judge Pickard's ruling went in our favour and stated that SAFA had been negligent by not supporting us, the bona fide affiliate women's football association. I was glad we had won but still not altogether satisfied. I wanted SAWFA to be reinstated as the pre-eminent body that represented women's football, but the ruling fell short of that. With the legal case over, the commission report was placed in a bottom drawer in some SAFA office and quickly forgotten. I still have a verbatim transcript copy of the proceedings if anyone would like to see it.

We had won, but it proved to be a hollow victory because the commission's main recommendation was to hold an election for members of the new board. What a farce. The tiny SAWFA board had no chance against the underhand tactics of the crisis committee who came mob-handed with jumped-up representatives from nonexistent regions. We were defeated. These people from outside the game, some of whom we had never heard of and who had never shown an interest in women's football, took over the running of the game. I use the term 'running' loosely because subsequently they achieved nothing and the president they appointed soon got bored and left, probably because there were no easy pickings.

However, I wasn't going away quietly. I decided to sue SAFA for negligence—amongst other things. After all, the Pickard Commission had ruled in our favour, so I intended to use the law to our advantage. Sean, a legal eagle cousin of mine, happened to be staying with me at the time and we put our heads together to plan a strategy. Even though his specialty was shipping law, I was not to be deterred—I had to use every tool at my disposal. The law is the law. Together we drew up a lengthy document that described how SAFA sidelined SAWFA and stripped us of any influence. This took months of running up and down to the Supreme Court, writing detailed analyses of contracts and agreements, learning strange (to me) legal terminology, and the whole rigmarole. It was also taking its toll on my levels of stress as I was juggling too many roles, including becoming more involved with indoor soccer, and for a while acting as president of the ruling body.

Finally, once my cousin Sean and I believed our case was airtight, we lodged it at the Supreme Court in Johannesburg. Our case was accepted. I knew I had a good chance of winning as I had my facts straight and knew where the opposition were weakest. I was now looking forward to the court battle ahead.

The SAFA board members were shocked when they were served the court documents. Now they knew I meant business. They could see that I wasn't going to melt away into the background and that I believed passionately in the principled development of the women's game.

The last thing they wanted was a public court case that would attract all the wrong headlines for the new-ish organisation. Consequently, shortly before the case was due to be heard, SAFA sent their lawyer Pooby Govindasamy to my house to plead with me to withdraw the case on the understanding that they would attend to all the matters of concern. In a word: appeasement. He even brought a prepared document of withdrawal to sign. What to do? Could I trust them at their word? I talked it over with Sean and we considered all the angles. The upshot was that we agreed I should sign and withdraw the case.

To this day I'm not sure if I did the right thing. According to the SAFA constitution, I was not allowed to take them to court, but if I abandoned the case would SAFA really accede to my reasonable demands? Either way I felt that if I pursued the case I could be the biggest loser in the end, so we stood down. SAFA and I agreed a truce and the two bodies came to an understanding about the administration of women's football.

Coincidentally at about this time FIFA came up with a ruling that women's football must be represented by a standing committee in each national federation, and not merely be an affiliate member. This time SAFA had no choice; when FIFA say 'Jump' national federations ask 'How high?' In 1999 a committee was put in place composed of powerful women from the world of football, including the owner of Mamelodi Sundowns, Anastasia Tsichlas, and Ria Stars supremo Ria Ledwaba. The committee also included women from other fields, such as sports administrators Kedi Tshoma and Josina Tellie. I saw this as a step in the right direction and had faith that they would plan a reasonable path forward.

I saw the women's committee as a step in the right direction, but my name was still mud in certain quarters. Hilton-Smith spelled trouble. At a subsequent SAFA workshop called "Walls to Bridges", Morewa's pal Oliphant tried to get rid of me, but big boss Irvin Khoza (co-founder of the PSL) stood up for me and said that I must remain in football. Respect. Stix Morewa resigned soon after due to the findings of the Pickard Commission, which painted him in a bad light not only with regards to women's football but also because of murky issues involving sponsorships and financial mismanagement.

Perhaps there was some justice after all.

Clearly the SAFA board had a change of heart about our falling-out because later they offered me a job, so some good came out of it, and it beat working out of the boot of my car, which I had been doing for the past twenty years. I even stood for president of the SAFA NEC—hard to believe considering the history, but true. I lost the vote (of course) but I had held my ground and proved a point—nothing is impossible if you believe in what you do.

9

BIRTH OF BANYANA

After the Pickard Commission ended in 1995, I was exhausted with all the politicking and stayed away from SAFA for a year or two. Sportswear company Reebok took me on part-time to lead coaching courses for women, mainly teachers, in various locations around the country. It was great fun travelling with the likes of Gloria Hlalele, Sam Mbatha and Themba Ngwenya, and the late Thuli Nkosi.

But just because I was no longer part of the national football federation didn't mean my burning ambition to attend a women's World Cup tournament had subsided; in fact it had grown. The 1995 tournament in Sweden was approaching and I had to find a way to get there.

The South African team would not be going to the tournament after coach Sandile Bali 'led' the team to an ignominious 11–2 defeat in the deciding two-leg qualifier with our old rivals Nigeria: 4–1 away and 1–7 at home.

The Nigeria match at the Rand stadium will forever be remembered for the understandably irate home spectators who pelted him with bottles. Only a wire fence saved him from being seriously injured. These were the days when there was only one African place in the finals. Later, after I joined FIFA, I complained at every meeting that one place for Africa was insufficient. Eventually they relented and awarded Africa a second place.

My parents were staying in an old age home at the time and luckily one of the residents had a son who lived in Sweden who kindly organised for me to stay with him. So off I flew, my first time out of the country since 1970, not sure where I was going to stay half the time. I spent some time with my contact, then hiked and backpacked my way to the venues around Sweden, mostly staying in camp sites. In one, I saw two black ladies. I secretly hoped they may be South Africans, so I immediately went up to say hello. They turned out to be English nonidentical twins of Nigerian descent, complete with strong 'limey' accents: Kehinde and Taiwo. They were also backpacking around the World Cup venues. They said they were friends with the then England team captain, Hope Powell. We decided to stick together and travelled to the England games together. It was great to have a little company to cheer on the teams.

After Norway lifted the trophy, we went our separate ways. Years later, when by chance I became friends with Hope through her work as a FIFA instructor, I mentioned the twins. It turned out she was still in touch with them and we all reignited our friendship. They even came out to South Africa to watch the African Women's Championship and wrote a book about their experiences. I returned from the World Cup fired up and, even though I was not officially employed by SAFA, ready to do anything I could to build the national squad.

BIRTH OF BANYANA

For the next three years South African women's soccer was stagnant—no inter-provincials were held during the 1997–98 seasons—until Banyana Banyana qualified for the 1998 African Women's Championship in Nigeria. Suddenly everything took off. The bad blood that emerged during the Pickard Commission was clearly forgotten by the SAFA board because my expertise was requested once again when I was offered the job of technical advisor, which entailed a lot of hands-on training with the teams and technical advice to the new coach, Nomalungelo Mooi. Nomsa Nkuna came in as team psychologist and Mary-Jane Sokela took over as team manager when Dara was offered a job at Reebok.

From February 1998 until the championship began in October we were intent on getting match fit. To this end the team travelled to Swaziland, Morocco, England (where we played Arsenal), Egypt and Kenya, where we played the national teams. Mozambique also sent a team to play us at home.

But in truth there was little time to bed in new players and build the team that I had always imagined Banyana Banyana could be. Despite the friendlies and all the hard training, the team was not fully prepared for the tournament and lost both group games—4–0 to Ghana and 3–2 to Cameroon—and did not advance to the knockout stage. Coach Nomalungelo Mooi then left because her mandate had been to qualify for the World Cup, which she had failed to do.

Now that I was back in the thick of things, I decided the women's team needed a stronger identity, something that would translate well to the terraces as well as in the press and on TV. The men's team were called Bafana Bafana (the boys or men), so we wanted something similarly catchy. After consultation with some of my black women colleagues, I came up with the name Banyana Banyana (the women, in loose translation) as a nickname for the women's senior team. I also came up with the names for the under-20 side (Basetsana, or the girls) and Bantwana for the under-17s (young girls).

With Mooi now gone, out of the blue I was offered the job of Banyana Banyana coach. I had finally got the job I'd always coveted. Now it was my responsibility to get the team ready for a big year in 2000 when South Africa was due to host the CAF African Women's Championship. I had to put into practice all the training I had received and prove that Banyana was a force to be reckoned with.

When my excitement abated a little, I realised the importance of this moment I had been working towards my whole adult life. All the bands and all the bikes and all the other sports I had indulged suddenly paled in comparison to the profound feeling of responsibility that now ran through my veins: Fran Hilton-Smith, coach, South Africa women's national football team. Now the work could begin.

Notwithstanding my optimism, I had always been aware of one serious blind spot in the team's performances—tactical awareness on the field. Natural talent and ambition will only take a team so far, so I enlisted the support of some of the top coaches in South Africa to help me: Farouk Khan, Ted Dumitru and Shakes Mashaba. I also had to get the team in peak physical condition for a gruelling tournament, so I also got sports scientists involved to aid training and build stamina.

Before that, however, there was an even bigger tournament coming up—the 1999 Women's World Cup, which would be hosted by the USA. With monotonous regularity, Nigeria once again qualified, together with the Black Queens of Ghana as the second team from the continent. The disappointment fuelled my two footballing ambitions: to beat Nigeria and to lead Banyana Banyana to their first World Cup.

For the record, the first of those ambitions would not be realised for another thirteen years, when we beat the Super Falcons 1–0 with a Janine van Wyk goal scored from the halfway line. South Africa beat Nigeria by the same score in the 2018 AFCON group stage in Ghana. Thembi Kgatlana scored. However, the joy was soured somewhat when Nigeria went on to beat us in the final.

Back to the 1999 World Cup in the USA... As national coach, I was part of a SAFA delegation that had been invited on an exchange programme with US Soccer. I later joined the US women's team in camp to study their tactics, but had to pay for myself. I scrimped and saved every penny for that trip, which was worth all the sacrifices because I was able to see women's football played on the biggest stage, and meet my footballing heroine, Michelle Akers. She was once again on the cup-winning side, even though she played with a dislocated shoulder. This was her last World Cup due to persistent injuries, so I was lucky to see one of the all-time greats before she retired. I will never forget that historic final when the USA beat China at the Rose Bowl with 90,000 frenzied spectators. Bizarrely, for a South African fan, it appeared that women's soccer in the USA was more popular than the men's game. Why couldn't we reach those heights at home? It was a glimpse of what women's football could achieve and a taste of what Banyana Banyana could look forward to when and if they ever qualified for the finals. One day, maybe.

I met up with Steve 'Kalamazoo' Mokone, who had moved to the USA and had always been a loyal ally of mine ever since he supported me at the SAFA workshop when Molefi Oliphant tried to get rid of me. Steve had been one of the first black South African players to ply his trade in Europe and beyond. He had a checkered past but became famous in the Netherlands in the 1950s as the first foreign professional, and even has a street and a football stand named after him. He was affectionately known as *die swarte meteor*, the black meteor, which was also the name of a novel and film based on his life. He retired to Washington DC and founded a foundation, of which I was a member. We kept in touch as he had a number of scholarships available for black players—both men and women—and wanted me to help him find suitable candidates.

Once more I returned fired up from a major tournament where South Africa was unrepresented. That's the thing about football, there's always another tournament to plan for. But there was no point doing what we had always done—to be successful I needed to widen my net of players.

Around this time I met a teenager called Janine van Wyk, a talented player who would later become captain of the national team. In 2020 she became the most capped South African player (male or female) and most capped female player on the continent.

Her path to becoming a South African sporting legend was not so predestined as it may appear. Janine's parents accompanied her to an early training session of mine at Johannesburg College of Education. Considering her traditional Afrikaner upbringing I was surprised she played soccer at all. I put the fifteen-year-old through her paces and it was immediately obvious to me that with the right guidance and encouragement she could become a great player. How had she become so proficient so young? For want of a woman's team, she had been playing in boys' teams since she was small (as I did as a youngster), and was encouraged by an uncle who had been a prominent player.

By this time there were not many teams left in the previously white neighbourhoods (in fact Janine had recently been turning out for Score Metals, a boys' team in

Germiston), and her nearest women's team was Springs Home Sweepers FC in Kwa-Thema township, which was led by Joseph Mkhonza. Janine was not fazed by the cultural shock of playing for a township team. She travelled there for both training and competitive matches every week, which was not an unchallenging trip for a young woman who was usually the only white on the pitch.

Around this time a colleague wrote to me and suggested I bring the Banyana team to Utah, USA, to play some college teams. The trip, arranged for April 2000, would be joint funded by our American hosts and SAFA. I jumped at the offer, and was especially pleased when Dara said she wanted to join the delegation (at her own expense). To my irritation was replaced as coach by Augusto Palacios for the tour. (I returned as coach to lead the team to the African Women's Championship later that year.)

I always found the Peruvian a bolshy man, barking instructions in a belligerent tone in broken English that often had the girls dropping their heads, with a predictable effect on their performance. He pushed the girls physically and had them up before sun-up to run around the streets of Edenvale. I never believed that jogging around the chilly streets, up and down uneven pavements, was good for either fitness or morale. Quality sleep is vital for athletes to recuperate and feel refreshed, so I couldn't see any benefits to the early morning regime. One winter's morning a player got knocked down by a cyclist on his way to work at around 5 a.m. I had to scrounge money from the petty cash to repair the cyclist's rear wheel.

Palacios once warned the team that if Peruvians lie or gossip ('gossit' as he pronounced it) hot coals would be placed on their tongues! Lovely.

This bellicose style was the polar opposite of mine. By this time I had developed my own brand of coaching that relied more on ball skills than endless physical work-outs, which do not improve mental focus when it comes to playing the game.

From a young age I was always hungry to learn about football tactics, an attitude I continued later in life. I was glued to the football channels on TV that showed the English Premier League, Italian Serie A and Spanish La Liga. I closely followed the different teams and major football nations to understand what tactics they used and what I could use in my own coaching career. People who came to my house often wondered if my TV showed any other channels.

One thing I was sure about was that training should be a reflection of the upcoming game. There was no point leaving all your best moves on the training ground; the training should be evident in the actual match.

I also became a great believer in promoting players with natural skills. Football, like all high-level sport, is a creative act, so allowing players to express themselves on the pitch is crucial to getting the best out of the team. In an 11 v 11 game, some players can play for long stretches and not even touch the ball. Great improvements can be made in small-sided training games, such as one against one, 2 v 2, 3 v 2, or even 5 v 2, as it honed players' individual skills and techniques that could be utilised in the wider tactical approach to matches.

My teams spent a huge amount of time on set plays—corners, free kicks, throw-ins, and the dreaded penalties, with substitutes shadowing behind the first choice player. I always tried to have two or three tactical options to call on for each set play. A pre-agreed signal would start a movement that would fool the opposition and enable us to score, or at least keep possession and advance up the field to launch an attack. This would give players options to solve problems and think for the team.

I tried to roll out this approach to training across all the women's national teams to adopt a uniform philosophy so that the under-17s could naturally progress to the under-20 squad and then on to Banyana Banyana. This was easier said than done, especially when there were different coaches for different squads with their own training regime and team tactics.

Anyway, as always my priority was to give Banyana as much quality training as possible, so despite the change of personnel we all looked forward to going to the USA.

It was snowing in Utah, which is common if you lived in Salt Lake City, but certainly not if you were used to the warmth of Gauteng. The players were frozen before, during and after matches! Despite the cold, the tour was a great learning experience for the girls and the team staff. We were all privy to their tactics, training regime and the whole support structure for the sport, which put ours in the shade. We played Brigham Young University (twice) and Weber State University, and lost all three matches. USA college teams act as feeders for the national squad; indeed, some of the teams we played against fielded players from the Stars and Stripes, so our girls were up against top competition. Despite the results on the field, the short international tour proved invaluable in preparing the team for future high-level tournaments.

The American hospitality was also in evidence. We were put up in a nice hotel that asked us to put our boots outside the doors after training so they could be rinsed, dried and polished. The players were dubious; in South Africa putting anything outside meant they would never be seen again. There was also an indoor heated swimming pool that the players gleefully jumped into after training. We visited the Salt Lake City winter Olympics site, and also the Mormon church capital buildings, which were incredible where we heard the resident choir which was amazing. All wonderful memories for the girls.

Later that year the CAF African Women's Championship came to South Africa for the first time, based in Vosloorus, south of Boksburg. I was brought back as coach. All the big African women's teams were there including Nigeria, Ghana and Cameroon, our three arch rivals. Unfortunately the tournament made world headlines for all the wrong reasons.

It all started so effortlessly for the home team. Without hardly breaking sweat, we progressed swiftly through the group stage, beating Réunion 3–0, Uganda 3–0 and Zimbabwe 2–1. In the semi-final we beat Ghana 1–0 with a Jo-Anne Solomons goal in the 9th minute, our most significant victory to date against the physically superior Black Queens. In the other semi-final, the Super Falcons rather ominously thrashed Zimbabwe 6–0.

So, South Africa v Nigeria in the final, at home.

This was the match I had imagined, planned and wished for. It seemed like the stars were lining up for one wonderful moment of glory. Now it was up to the girls.

The stadium was crammed. In fact there were many more spectators than there were seats. That should have been expected because women's games were still free, and with the home team in the final, the stadium was a magnet for anyone looking for a party. Even Winnie Mandela showed up with a huge entourage of security who squeezed into the already packed VIP section.

After a tough start for Banyana Banyana, Nigeria scored in the 30th minute: 0–1. We improved as the game progressed and in the second half, for once, were holding the Super Falcons and making plenty of attacking plays into their half. We were only a goal down and I had the feeling that this would be Banyana Banyana's moment. This would justify all the sacrifices and indifference over the years; for the first time we were going to bring the AFCON trophy home to South Africa.

But football rarely plays out the way you expect. In the 73rd minute there was a one-on-one in our 18-yard box. Our defender went in for the tackle but came off worst and ended up on the ground in a heap, injured. The ball bounced to another advancing Nigerian player as our goalkeeper came out, but she was impeded by our prone player. The striker passed the player on the ground and got off a shot. The ball went into the net: 0–2. But the crowd made their own judgment about the legitimacy of the goal. They decided that the Nigerian striker was offside and the player on the ground had obstructed our keeper, so the goal should not stand.

Shouts of derision and threats were heard to ring around the stadium, which grew and grew and soon turned into fighting between the angry home supporters and the Nigerian fans who were still singing and cheering in celebration of the second goal. The South African fans were soon riled up to fever pitch.

Most of the Nigerian spectators were sitting together on the stand above the changing room tunnel which, unusually, was opposite the main grandstand and the team benches. This made them a contained target. The home fans stormed the stand and a full-on pitched battle broke out. It quickly spread like a virus throughout the stadium where pockets of fighting erupted and groups of people started running away or mistakenly heading towards trouble. It was mayhem. The South African fans started throwing bricks and stones at the Nigerians (where they got them from I don't know), which they returned with some of their own.

After inciting the crowd by exaggeratedly celebrating the goal, the Nigerian goalkeeper Ann Chiejene soon learned how the Banyana Banyana fans felt about that—with rocks that were fired towards her goal. She ran out of the 18-yard box to show the referee the stones that had been thrown, and refused to return to the goal. Meanwhile the game had restarted even though many of the missiles were raining down on the players. When the ball went out of play the Super Falcons, willing the game to be over, huddled together in shock in the centre of the pitch.

The Nigerians were not the only ones running scared. My players and staff all feared for their lives. We couldn't get to the dressing rooms as that was where the worst fighting was taking place. The main grandstand behind us was packed to capacity so we couldn't escape that way and in any case new fights were breaking out all over. Mostly innocent people were caught in the crossfire, including children, but parents didn't know what to do for the best. Nor did we.

The game was abandoned, but we had nowhere to run and so we all joined the players in the centre circle. The few police and security officers were quickly overwhelmed by the mayhem and could do nothing to control the crowd. Panic set in amongst the peaceful fans—moms and dads and children—who then tried to make a run for it by climbing over a high fence that surrounded the stadium, as if escaping a warzone.

We could hear some of the so-called fans who got out of the stadium venting their anger by smashing the cars parked outside. There was barely an intact windscreen left in the car park. Reinforcements finally arrived and the police started dispersing the crowd with tear gas, but the damage was done—to the stadium, to the Nigerian fans, and to our international reputation. Nigeria was awarded the game. The chaos, captured in excruciating close-up on TV, made all the newspapers next morning.

The sports history books and websites will forever list the game as "South Africa 0– Nigeria 2 (abandoned)".

BIRTH OF BANYANA

Unfortunately the championship in 2000 was not a World Cup qualifier event, and the lack of consistent competition resulted in the team once more failing to qualify for the 2003 World Cup. Without international friendlies a team will never reach their potential. With the USA playing around 130 friendlies in the early 2000's and Banyana Banyana playing one or two, as did many other top African teams, lack of competition was a serious stumbling block, even for the teams that qualified for the World Cup. Lack of sponsorship was another big problem. It costs a significant amount of money to train and equip a squad of players and then travel to play your opponents. It was a vicious circle: no money, no friendlies, no match fitness, no qualification.

During 2000 there was another huge disappointment for South African football. SAFA had put together a bid to host the 2006 (men's) World Cup. The South African bid team were all confident and the feedback from the twenty-four FIFA delegates was very positive. Even though our main competition came from the German bid, everything pointed to the first World Cup being held in Africa in 2006.

Dara and I went to watch the draw at some fancy conference room at the Sandton Sun hotel. The sense of excitement and expectation was palpable. Finally it was time to watch the announcement live from Zürich. FIFA President Sepp Blatter stepped onto the stage, opened the envelope, and said, 'The winner is... Deutschland!'

Dara and I looked at each other, speechless. I looked around looking for an explanation of some kind; we were all devastated. Everyone at SAFA believed that this was our time, and after the announcement the entire room collectively felt that something had been stolen from us. It was later revealed that in the final round of voting, the New Zealand candidate Charlie Dempsey (who had been instructed by his own federation to vote *for* South Africa) had abstained, allowing Germany to win the vote 12–11.

Dempsey said that he had been given a free hand to vote as he saw fit, and that he had abstained from voting because of the intolerable pressure from supporters of both the German and South African bids, and because of the attempts to bribe him. FIFA rejected calls for a new vote, and opened an internal inquiry into the allegations of corruption. Following widespread criticism of his decision to abstain, he stood down from his role later that year.

The year 2000 was also memorable for a great personal disappointment. After the best part of two years as national coach, in his great wisdom SAFA president Molefi Olifant moved me out of coaching and handed me the role of national teams manager. Effectively I was relieved of all technical aspects of the team—for which I was eminently qualified—and made responsible for administration of the women's game. I was mad as a snake. As coach, with a good backroom team around me and some great players, I had managed to return Banyana Banyana to the top table of African football by leading them to the African Women's Championship final (one of five occasions when we were losing finalists). I had also begun the restructuring of the team and led the adoption of new tactics that I was sure would help us qualify for the 2003 World Cup finals in the USA.

The nice trophy I received at the SAFA annual awards in 2000 in recognition of my contribution to coaching did little to assuage my disappointment at losing my job. But my anger was tempered somewhat by a phone call I received out of the blue soon after from an official at FIFA, which was destined to change my life. I will come to that shortly.

Regular competition is not the only way that African teams should prepare for big games. Less threatening than stadium riots but nonetheless equally controversial, there are other ways that team officials can bend the rules to gain advantage. At this time I was also coaching Basetsana, the under-20 girls national team. In our debut attempt to qualify for the African championship we lost, of course, to Nigeria who, it was obvious to anyone with eyes, fielded overage players, which had become a common cheat in the girls' game. Boys' ages can usually be indicated by MRI scans of the wrist, which determines bone growth, but the test is less accurate in women, so is not used. Federations from Nigeria, Cameroon and other countries took advantage of this grey area and organised passports for girls en masse that showed the 'acceptable' age. If the passport said the girls were all aged under nineteen then we had to accept it. End of story.

Another time, in the Central African Republic for an under-20s match, the opposition team declaration showed that all their players were born on the same day. Some of the older girls/women even had crow's feet wrinkles around their eyes. Later, coach Vera Pauw, assistant coach Lizbeth Michelsen and I did some intensive research on the Nigerian team and, with help from a Nigerian defector, we obtained birth certificates that showed players' ages differed from their faked passports. I protested many times and sent documents to CAF and FIFA, but nothing came of it. Without scientific testing the problem will not be solved easily.

The Central African Republic was, and still is, a difficult place to get to. For the fixture mentioned above, SAFA had to hire a private jet for the nine-hour trip. Appropriately the company was called Millionaire Jets, because it cost R1million to hire the plane for the return journey. For once the under-20s squad of around twenty-three had plenty of space to bed down on the sixty-seater plane. We had to take all the food we required and left half on the plane ready for the return trip. After the match (playing against the oldest teens on the continent), we returned to the airport to discover someone had broken into the plane and stolen all the supplies.

Cultural practices can also play a big part in both men's and women's football when teams have a mix of ethnicities and backgrounds. Some of these practices assume significance, shall we say, beyond scientific explanation. The men's national squad, Bafana Bafana, especially had a lot of rituals before games, some taken to the extreme. For white players, and for some black, this was often hard to accept, especially for Christians. For instance, the team jerseys would be taken away the night before a match to be 'treated' by a Sangoma who would perform various rituals over the kit. Players would also drink various concoctions to counteract the power of the opponents. Herbs were burned in the changing rooms and players were asked to jump over burning branches. This caused havoc at the World Cup games as it set off the fire alarms. We once had a team manager and a coach who polished the girls' boots with a special compound the night before the games. Some of the girls objected and would bring a second pair to wear on match day.

My best story of the clash between modern medicine and cultural beliefs occurred at a Banyana Banyana training camp in preparation for an important qualifier. One of our strikers hurt her knee, which was so swollen she had to use crutches. We had a big game coming up and I couldn't afford to lose her. The team doctor Dimikatso and physiotherapist Carin were both working day and night to get her match fit, spending hours on ultrasound treatment and nurturing the player to fitness.

At lunchtime on the day before the crucial match the player sneaked out of camp and went to a Sangoma in

Soweto to heal the knee the 'traditional' way. He made a number of small incisions around the knee then, using a halved tennis ball, sucked out the seemingly offensive fluid that he believed was causing the problem. Next thing we know, the player arrived back at camp for training, minus crutches, walking around happily with a row of open incisions around her knee. Of course the doctor and physio went ballistic as they now couldn't use the physio machines in case the pre-treatment gel entered the open wounds. From this unhappy outcome we made a new rule —when in camp, the players had to report only to the team doctor for treatment. When they were at home they could follow any practice they liked. And probably did.

Another practice used throughout Africa is to pour various kinds of *muti* on the field, especially in and around the goalposts, a practice intended to prevent the opposition from scoring. Some teams also surreptitiously buried items on the field, but with the advent of synthetic grass this caused a number of problems after the playing surface was damaged and burnt.

If *muti* and the Sangoma's potency proved ineffectual the players could always resort to singing and praying before a match. These fortifying rituals were an important part of the warm-up. The loud singing was also meant to intimidate the opponents in the neighbouring dressing room. Occasionally African opponents resorted to the same tactic and the two teams would try to out sing each other, producing a cacophony of noise. This could really alarm European opponents at international games, especially when Banyana Banyana broke into song in the tunnel just before taking to the field. It was enough to unsettle even the most confident teams.

Fairy ballerina, aged seven

Biker jacket

Libra biker gang

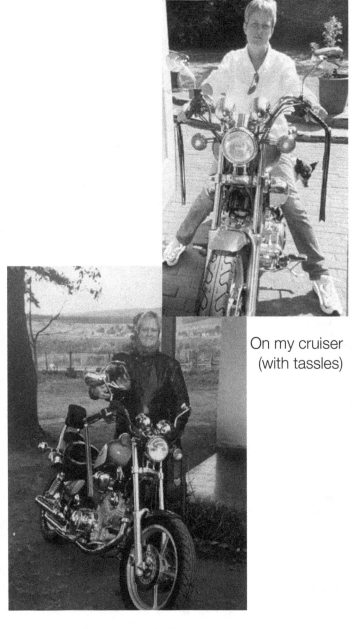

On my cruiser
(with tassles)

Graskop, 2005

Spirit 2, 1997

Basadi gig, 2006

Basadi Women of Jazz

First national women's team, 1993

In the stern of the ladies coxed 4

High Performance Centre, class of 2016

2010

FIFA coaching course, Iran, 2003

FIFA coaching course, Nigeria, 2012

Fran meets her hero, Nelson Mandela

Scouting for new players from the touchline

Level 2 coaching course, 2014-15

Send-off for u-17s to 2018 World Cup in Uruguay

Nigeria, before we came across cannibals

FIFA Task Force, 2015

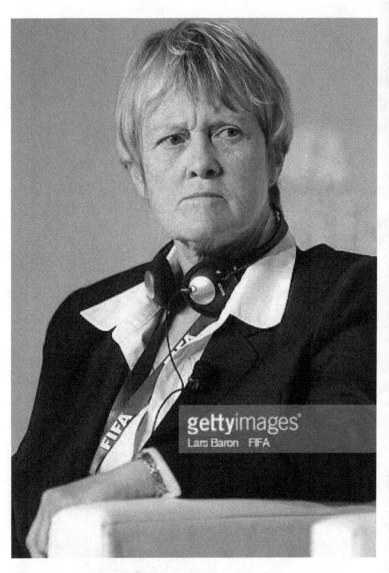

On serious FIFA business
(Photo by Lars Baron - FIFA/FIFA via Getty Images)

10

NAIJA

During my fifty years in football I have travelled to many countries in Africa, either as player, coach or manager of various national women's teams and later as a FIFA match official. Over that time I came to realise how blessed South Africa was on this amazing continent. While our country has faced huge infrastructure challenges since we got rid of apartheid, generally speaking, from plumbing to pizza, from burgers to banking, things just seem to work better here. No wonder we are viewed as the land of milk and honey by some. The home countries—those that border RSA—seem to feed off our culture, economy and lifestyles, but only once you push on into central Africa, to Republic of Congo, DR Congo, Equatorial Guinea, Cameroon, etc., can you say that you've experienced the real Africa.

So if you want some full-on African action you have to travel to the central belt of the continent or West Africa where there is one sport that unites us all: football. The more you travel the more you realise it is not just a sport; it is a language, a form of communication, a profound shared experience—and heaven knows we need a few more of those these days.

Within the family of football there is one country I must explore in more detail, one that plays by a different set of rules—in lifestyle, in business, and in their approach to sporting excellence: Nigeria, locally known as Naija. You cannot be taken seriously in the world of African women's soccer without taking on the footballing superpower of the Super Falcons. They are by far the continent's most successful team, having won the Africa Women's Cup of Nations eleven times. (For heaven's sake, it's only been held thirteen times!) There are a few good reasons for their success, some sporting, some not so sporting, which I shall come to in good time.

As I have already mentioned in passing, it is with some personal regret that Banyana Banyana never won the title under my tenure, although we were runners-up five times —on three occasions losing to the Super Falcons. So you could say that Nigeria has featured large in my footballing life.

At one time Banyana Banyana were scared of the Nigerian women's team; there is no other way to describe how we felt in our first few encounters. Physically we were no match at any age for the Nigerian players. Just seeing them line up next to our girls during the pre-match rituals made us realise that, compared to our relatively svelte players, they were hewn from black granite. Their girls were fearsome looking—strong, wiry and naturally athletic. One of their all-time stars, Mercy Akide, was the most naturally athletic player I have ever encountered.

She lives and coaches in America and we remain friends to this day.

Of course their remarkable physiques are largely down to good genes, but I always wondered whether their diet of yams and roots helped produce these fine looking players. I recently asked a former Nigerian international what they ate and my assumption that they were fuelled by healthy food freshly grown and pounded was correct—*garri* (pounded cassava) and *fufu* (a mixture of cassava and green plantain) are mainstays of their diet. No junk food for the Super Falcons then.

Not content with being physically imposing, there were other challenges to playing the African champions. The first of which was wondering whether the opposition's under-17 side were actually under the age of seventeen. This went for the under-20 games too. As I have mentioned, officials from opposing teams (this was not an exclusively Nigerian tactic) would forge documents for their players who, off the record, had no qualms telling our players their correct ages. As there was no foolproof method of age testing—and still isn't as I write in 2021—we could never prove they were over age, even though some were obviously so. My sixteen-year-olds would come off the field at halftime battered and bruised after clashing with fully grown, honed adults. We almost always lost these contests. The occasional draw was a great result for us.

Despite my reservations about their commitment to fair play, and my baptism of fire in the West African school of hard knocks, it was only in later years when I revisited Nigeria to lead a FIFA coaching course with many of the former players that I realised what terrific people they were. I learned how they were able to create a menacing façade when on the playing field that put the fear of God into allcomers. It certainly had the desired effect on our teams. Notwithstanding the many anecdotes

I shall tell of hardship or unfairness, of confusion and, occasionally, blind terror, from this vantage point I can honestly say that I have come to terms with many aspects of Nigeria and still have many friends there to this day.

That said, in the early days it wasn't all sweetness and light. It is hard to know where to begin to describe my trips to the country during the late 1990s and most of 2000 with the three women's national teams. The first word that comes to mind is 'nightmare'. I promise every single word is true, even though the dates and names of some venues may not correlate exactly—probably because I have tried to erase them from my memory bank. To this day, the delta states of Warri, Kaduna and Oghara are names that still send a shiver down my fused spine.

With a population of somewhere north of 206 million (and counting), Nigeria has a marvellously diverse landscape, much of which is dense jungle with temperatures that often exceed 45 degrees Celcius, with humidity from hell—that is, when it's not raining. When it rains it's a mudbath.

I will never forget my first visit to Lagos, a teeming city of millions of loud, curious, colourfully dressed people who, it always seemed to me, all wanted to be on the exact square metre of roadway where I was standing. Let's just say that they have a different attitude to personal space. No social distancing there. I remember my first walk around the city; pedestrians were ten deep on either side of the road, half of whom were trying to sell stuff to the other half. Most women had basins on their heads: one would be selling cheap kitchen wares, the next selling dusty clothes, another selling sweating food. It looked like a cross between a gigantic mobile yard sale and a refugee crisis. The markets were so crammed it was difficult to catch a breath, and I could hardly see the sky because of all the electric cables and phone lines running every which way overhead. This was where I learned about hot-wiring, where the whole neighbourhood connected their electricity supply to a single legitimate cable that was being paid for by one unsuspecting neighbour.

And the traffic! I have never experienced anything like it. It would take us an hour in a mini-bus to travel one kilometre in the city centre. The highways were not much better, even the double-decker motorways crawled along. As the traffic moved so slowly, vendors were able to walk up and down between lanes selling their indispensable street food. Some I recognised, some I had no clue. Cooked items on sticks could have been anything—rats? bats? bush meat?

But of course before you hit the city you have to negotiate arrival at Lagos Murtala Muhammed International Airport, a teeming place with hundreds of people milling around—some travelling, some loitering, some on the make—which made even the simplest tasks tiresome. When we emerged from the terminal we were hit by a wall of heat as if someone had opened an oven door. Even people who never sweated, like me, would leak from every pore.

Sometimes the biggest challenge for these international games was simply getting to the venue. On one flight to Nigeria the plane stopped in Gabon to pick up some connecting passengers. We all trooped off to the terminal building and sat waiting patiently looking out at the stationary plane on the tarmac. There didn't seem to be an awful lot of activity, and I was soon to learn why. We were informed that there was no fuel for the plane and we would have to wait for a delivery tanker. We sat for hours with no indication of a possible departure time. The players were getting hungry and thirsty and SAFA had given me precious little petty cash, believing I would not need it on the relatively short journey. I found some Madeira cakes and a few bottles of water for sale at a kiosk and did my best to share it amongst the team. After *ten hours* the plane was finally ready for boarding. At the announcement, all the other passengers—both from the original flight and the connecting passengers—started lining up at the gate. It became immediately plain that there were more people in the queue than seats on the plane. Having learned some hard lessons of African travel, I was concerned that not all of these people had tickets, so I suggested to my officials and security that we make a chain at the front of the queue to ensure all the players and staff got on board. As the flight staff opened check-in there was an immediate surge to get on the plane—it was clear they operated a first come first served policy whether or not passengers had a ticket. We had to hold firm to ensure we all got on and then we ran across the tarmac to the waiting aircraft and scampered on.

The return journey was no easier. I seemed to age unnaturally every time we had to fly home from Nigeria because we nearly always arrived lastminute.com at the airport for the twice-a-week flights—if we missed the flight we were stumped. Match officials would disappear after meeting their obligations to get us to the airport, so Lord knows what we would have done for days on end stranded in some forgettable location that we wouldn't have necessarily chosen as a holiday destination.

Our flights were often booked through the official SAFA travel agency, FliAfrica. Our contact, a guy called George, would always get the cheapest flights for us, which usually meant flying via who-knows-where to get to our destination, rather than direct. Nairobi was a popular choice as a connection because it was a large hub airport and seemed to be midway between us and most other African destinations. The only drawback was that, during my time visiting the lesser known airport terminals of the continent, Kenya Airways invariably cancelled our onward flights for unspecified reasons. I consequently spent far too many nights sleeping on terminal floors surrounded by players waiting for the aeroplane that may or may not show up the following day. One time—a new low point—the then SAFA president Kirsten Nematandani slept next to me on the floor. (This was pre-2016, before he was found guilty of violating FIFA's Code of Ethics and banned for five years.) Eventually I got wise to the FliAfrica rep George who was booking us onto tortuously difficult travel itineraries either to milk the system or because he had no clue of the impact the disrupted travel would have on the players. On one occasion I insisted he travel with the team on the Gabon flight to experience his own travel arrangements. He got the picture, and never did it again.

Lagos Murtala Airport may have been a hair-raising mob scene but the domestic airport terminal was in a league of its own. I say terminal but that gives the impression of an airy, purposeful place with the emphasis on jet travel. Far from it. Dark and dingy just about covers it. Not what you want in a departure terminal. The shambolic room could hold no more than fifty people and was always jam packed. What little petty cash I was allowed by SAFA would have to be saved for real emergencies such as paying bribes to baggage handlers to ensure our luggage actually got on the little plane—the one whose safety record always worried me. Inside, the aircraft was a menagerie. That's not an exaggeration. Chickens and other small animals were allowed on the packed to capacity domestic flights and I would often share the row with passengers who insisted on sharing their huge plastic shopping bags with my lap.

On one flight, in a plane that probably shouldn't have taken to the skies, I flew with our then national coach Joseph 'Skesh' Mkhonza who hated flying at the best of times. The pilot switched on what was supposed to be the air conditioner, which everyone was praying for because it was 45 degrees. But instead of cool, pure air coming through the vents, strange hazy clouds of water droplets started pouring out of the side panels, enveloping us all. Soon we could hardly see the other end of the aircraft; it looked like the plane was covered in smoke. Poor Skesh nearly had a heart attack; he was jumping up and down and moaning that the end was nigh. Meanwhile the two pilots upfront, who we could see through the open cockpit door, had little fans blowing cool air on their faces, oblivious to their passengers' distress. The plane was so small that all our luggage, including a large steel trunk full of our kit that we schlepped everywhere, had to fly on a different plane. I was more than a little concerned that it would not arrive at our destination. It did, *just* before the game. After that I made the girls carry their boots in their backpacks.

Another time we were returning from an outlying town to Lagos for our onward flight home to Johannesburg. It was the usual bun fight at departures and everyone was keener than ever to get a seat on the plane. As I was watching the queue ahead slowly moving, I saw what appeared to be money changing hands with the officials who stood at the bottom of the aircraft steps. I noted that something unusual was happening but let it pass. I was the first of our squad to get onboard, which was my usual strategy, to check out seating arrangements inside the plane before my players got on. Seats were never reserved in Nigeria so we had to make the best of it. I got the players seated, or so I thought. On doing a head count I realised that not everyone was onboard, yet the plane was already full. I rushed to the aircraft door and spotted eight of our party still on the runway being refused permission to board. Then the penny dropped: the exchange of money I had seen earlier was from people buying tickets from the official on the tarmac to board the already full flight. There were no checks at the departure door so it was easy for someone to wander onto the tarmac and get into the queue to take a seat that had already been sold. Our SAFA head of delegation, Ace Kika, was shouting and performing on the runway that the whole team had to board the flight to make our connection back to Johannesburg. What on earth would the forgotten eight have done in the remote, provincial town? All the Nigerian Football Federation (NFF) officials had long gone and I had no way of contacting them. Horrors.

By now a few idling soldiers took an interest in proceedings and had made an appearance, brandishing guns around in their trademark I'm-in-charge gesture. I was shouting down the steps to let the rest of our party board and insisting the pilot could not fly without the rest of my group. Ace had by now taken to standing in front of the plane with his arms up yelling that the plane can't go without them. The soldiers, not knowing the full story but getting jittery at the commotion, now aimed their guns at him rather menacingly. Meanwhile I was still negotiating with pilot and cabin crew. After much deliberation the rest of my squad were allowed on board but had to sit on crew seats and in the toilets. It was not exactly business class service, but we didn't care, at least we were all off to Lagos.

These team trips often felt more like adventures than preparations for international sporting events. We wanted to proudly represent our country, but it often seemed that we were hindered at every turn. Before leaving I would always request that someone from the South African consulate in Nigeria meet us at the airport to help us through customs and follow us to the destination to check on suitability. Most times they showed up. Our airport transfer pick-up would typically be in sixteen-seater buses —for up to twenty-four people plus equipment. Occasionally our hosts would provide a separate van for our gear but more often than not we would have to hold the balls, kit, luggage and medical supplies on our laps for hours on end.

Wherever the team went we were accompanied by a police or army escort known as Operation Fire, which may sound like the title of a shoot-em-up movie but was actually quite an accurate description in the circumstances. Operation Fire consisted of five or six fearsome soldiers or armed police in grey fatigues and helmets travelling in Jeeps or on *okadas* (small motorbikes). They all carried whips and firearms of varying descriptions, which they vigorously brandished, often shooting warning shots into the air if people didn't get out of the way quick enough.

Of course, the louder they announced our arrival the more curious were the thousands of people who came out to see what all the fuss was about, who were then quickly despatched with the crack of a whip across their backs. The spectators probably had little interest in a team of teenagers from South Africa kicking a ball around a pitch until our arrival was announced by gunfire and sirens, which stoked them into a frenzy.

The armed officers, individually known as cadres, would lash out at anyone in their path, often sending them sprawling off their little bikes. Once, a family of five—mother, father, three kids plus shopping—were balanced precariously on the seat, pillion, petrol tank and handlebars and doing their best to mind their own business until we arrived and our escort sent them reeling off into the bush. Move over, the under-20s are in town!

Another time we were driving on a narrow road to Kaduna, about 200 kms north of Abuja, when we got held up by a slower car in front. The soldiers began hooting and yelling at the driver to move over, but there was nowhere to move over *to*. No problem for the cadres. As the road widened a little, our driver forced their Jeep up alongside the little car and nudged it off the road down a steep decline. God knows, I hope the family within survived.

On yet another occasion we came up to a robot—not that they always worked—where a car driver was waiting for the green light so that he could cross the junction like a good citizen. A cadre jumped off the Jeep, ran up to the driver, put a machine gun against his head and demanded he move. *Now!* All the girls were holding their breath, probably wondering where on earth they had landed. *We came here to play the beautiful game,* they were thinking, *not take part in a war!* Meanwhile I was putting on a brave face as if to show them everything was under control. Far from it. Although I couldn't reveal it in front of the team, these unnecessary displays of machismo always terrified me.

During my time with Banyana Banyana, the team travelled to most of the thirty-six Nigerian states. So whenever we got into a bus we never knew when we might step out of it as we were driven to our team hotel the long way. Many of our games took place in what seemed to me to be the most out of the way destinations miles out of anything that might be called a town as a sly tactic to give us something else to worry about.

Our trips to Delta state on the Gulf of Guinea would entail travel on that rare curiosity in West Africa: a highway. But the highway would go only so far, then suddenly the tarmac would terminate in the middle of nowhere and the driver would have to cross the central reservation to the opposite carriageway and continue against the oncoming traffic. This never phased the driver who saw it as just another minor challenge in life's rich tapestry—as did the drivers coming towards us in the fast lane.

No matter who our driver was on these visits they were probably all took instruction from the same Wacky Races school of motoring and only knew one speed: somewhere between breakneck and white knuckle. The girls would be terrified, holding onto the seat cushions for dear life. No amount of complaining would slow the driver down. Our team psychologist Nomsa Nkuna would sit in front and, with a catch of panic in her voice, repeatedly request, 'Easy, driver, *easy!*' to no avail. Traffic accidents—and there were many—often meant the cars being abandoned and left to the local car-stripping vultures.

Another cause of upset was the sometimes comical accommodation we were booked into. The Nigerian hotels were something else. They clearly had a glut of tiles because every last reception, dining room and bedroom was tiled both wall to wall and up the walls. The bedrooms always featured a huge bed that was usually dressed in a 1970s nylon bedspread. I never understood the fascination with the big beds. Maybe they were meant for the whole family. (I suppose with more than 200 million people to cater for, that should go without saying.) Everything else was human-sized, such as the standard trickling shower—more an annoying drip than a convenient method to wash oneself; it's the only place I have had to walk around in a shower to get wet. And there was always a plastic bucket and basin so you could collect used water to throw over your body. To be fair, this was also intended for the Muslim pre-prayer ritual *wudhu*.

One time I was assigned a room in a plush Lagos hotel that had just been built. And I mean *just*. Clearly the man who should have corrected the snags had not yet been round because we walked into freshly painted bedrooms (as in still tacky), and doors that either refused to close or had a gap at the bottom large enough to let in a small dog. Windows were lopsided and made you feel rather dizzy. (*Is it me or does the outside world look off-balance?*) And, of course, the usual six-person bed built for the whole family, this time without a headboard.

I proceeded to the bathroom. I was chuffed to see that the brand new basin had lovely stylish taps—except that no water came out of them. I looked under the basin to discover there were no connecting pipes, just loose-fitting faucets. Shower? Ditto. Toilet? Thank heavens for small mercies. It flushed.

I compared my facilities with others in the squad—every room in the hotel was the same. So, thinking ahead to our training sessions over the next few days, I went off to find an official to enquire how the team were supposed to wash following their exertions on the training ground. I was taken to a location opposite the hotel and shown a large pipe on which was fitted a tap like a fire hydrant. This, I was informed, was our source of water for the duration. The response from my dumbfounded team was a collective look of incredulity. After training each day the players would have to gather around the makeshift water supply to fill a bucket of cold water to go wash.

So the first night I flopped into bed after the usual kind of first day on tour in Nigeria: I'd experienced an unnecessarily long two-connection flight, been picked up at the airport by a sixteen-seater bus for twenty-four of us, then driven through unnamed towns by a close relative of Lewis Hamilton—so I'm knackered and just want to close my eyes in the unfeasibly capacious bed. I mentioned the doors earlier, but it was only when it was time for lights out that I noticed there was no lock on the door into the communal hallway.

Next morning I was rudely awakened by two huge men who marched into the room carrying the missing headboard. I was lying in the bed just coming to, but quickly assumed a shocked look of distress. The two guys were not fazed in the least. With me still in the bed holding the sheet up to my chin, they proceeded to lift the large wooden headboard over my head and fit it to the wall behind me. There was not a glimmer of embarrassment or awkwardness from either of them. When the hammering stopped, they fixed the side lamps to the wall and connected all the cables. Then the two men disappeared as if they were never there—and nor was I—and no doubt moved along to the next guest down the hall.

On another visit to Nigeria I had to change some petty cash into local currency to buy bananas and water (and for once the players were looking forward to receiving a little pocket money). I asked the Nigerian official who was assigned to the team to take me to the bank. He looked a bit puzzled and explained that no one used banks in Lagos because their exchange rate was so poor. Where to then? The local money dealer.

As darkness fell I climbed onto the pillion seat of some unknown motorcyclist, and off we sped into Lagos. After riding around for a while we arrived at a large white tent on the side of the road. I entered. Money from top to bottom! I could not believe my eyes. It was like cashing-up time in a casino. I handed the man at the counter my limited amount of US dollars—they only changed USD—and he gave me a huge pile of naira in exchange. I could hardly fit the brick of cash into my bag. We then rode back to the camp where I counted out the players' money. They each got a big wad of bills and thought they were rich until they tried to buy something and realised the notes were worth very little.

This incident is indicative of the great divide between SAFA's attitude towards the men's and women's teams, which came into stark contrast whenever we played abroad. I understand that men's football is a worldwide money-spinner that attracts huge crowds and TV revenues, but it had to start somewhere, and over the past decades SAFA has learned to develop the sport into a big business. Now that strategies and processes are in place for the South African game, why not roll it out to the women's game? Recent women's World Cups have been hugely successful sporting events in terms of attendance at the games and TV viewing figures. But it seemed during my time that I was always shouting at deaf ears for support, encouragement, money and, it has to be said, respect.

The Bafana Bafana manager was given a credit card for his international trips, but the poor relation women's team manager was handed a paltry amount of petty cash and told to make the best of it. The men's team manager was allowed to go on pre-game inspection visits to check out overseas facilities in advance; no such luck for us. Take it or leave it was SAFA's attitude. Bafana sometimes flew in chartered planes and stayed in 5-star hotels while we made do with dodgy minibuses and seedy accommodation. Bafana would generally take a chef, but no chance for the ladies; more often than not we lived on rice and plantain as our main meal of the day.

One of the events in Nigeria I remember clearly was a 2004 Olympic qualification match against the Super Falcons. We were accommodated in a beautiful hotel in Lagos. It was so plush that I initially wondered if there had been a mix-up with our booking. While acknowledging to myself that this was a strange turn of events, I thought that maybe the tide had turned and we were finally being afforded some respect by our Nigerian hosts. In fact I was being blindsided. I was enjoying the relatively luxurious atmosphere a little too much and should have listened more closely to my intuition.

The day before the game we were given jugs of juice at mealtime, something we generally never drank. That afternoon and early evening all hell broke loose. A number of the players started collapsing with violent vomiting and diarrhoea. Seven of my key players were rushed to hospital and put on saline drips for dehydration. Not great preparation for an Olympic qualifier. I had to gather my troops and make a plan for the game the following day. Then the kit manager came down with the same illness, who was beside himself crying and screaming with the pain and distress of it all. The remaining players—what you might call the walking wounded—were sitting in the corridors petrified that they were next to be carted off to hospital.

Next morning I played Inspector Clouseau and asked other hotel guests, including some airline flight crews, if they had been given the same juice. No, just us. Of course, I cannot point the finger at any individual, but there is no doubt in my mind that we had been deliberately poisoned to ensure the Super Falcons would progress to the Olympics at our expense.

The following day, the few of us who were left standing had to report to the stadium before the match. We demanded a meeting with the Ghanaian match commissioner to inform him of our plight and voice our suspicions. Far from receiving a little sympathy, he could not have been less interested. He said that as we could field seven players (the minimum allowed by FIFA), the rules stipulated that we had to play. By this time I was also acting as an occasional match commissioner for FIFA and had fortunately brought the phone number of Walter Gagg, the FIFA official in charge of competitions. The squad knew that our situation was desperate and with only seven players we were heading for a drubbing at the hands of our great rivals. I told them that our last chance was to make the call to FIFA and request a stay of execution. We all gathered around the landline as I phoned Walter at his office in Switzerland and pleaded our case, stressing that even in the unlikely event that we were not deliberately poisoned, it was hardly sporting to allow an international fixture to continue under such circumstances. He agreed, and said the game should be postponed for a few days.

Meanwhile the 50,000-seater stadium was already full to the hilt, as Nigerian games usually were. The spectators had to be informed via the public address system that the game was off. As you might imagine, the thousands of supporters who had come to see the Super Falcons thrash Banyana Banyana were not amused. Soon we had a riot on our hands... well, actually we exited stage left as soon as possible. The per usual over-the-top police and military presence took the opportunity to unleash their whips, which were soon flying around like they were scything grain, and then guns started popping off and the water cannons were deployed. Hectic stuff.

Two days later a significant portion of our team was still in hospital, including our only two goalkeepers and our star striker, Portia Modise. We were running out of time; the pressure to host the rescheduled game was building. The match officials at the ground insisted that as we still had seven healthy players, the original ruling should stand and it was game on. We headed off to the full stadium not knowing how we were going to approach such a one-sided match—we hadn't even decided who we were going to put in goal. We continued to vociferously protest this ludicrous state of affairs until the match officials caved in and *again* postponed the game. This time the spectators were furious, and took it out on us by pelting our bus with rocks on our departure from the stadium, one of them breaking a window. This is how it's going to end, I thought, we're all going to be stoned to death! Luckily no one was injured. By this time our escorts must have been fed up with the postponements because all the usual police and military cadres and their vehicles were suddenly nowhere to be seen.

Two days later everyone was out of hospital and we played the game. With half a team of groggy, still recovering players we only lost 1–0. But more importantly our Olympic dreams were over for another four years.

When I got back to the SAFA office and complained about our treatment to Stix Morewa and Molefi Olifant, they said that we mustn't make a fuss—'that's Africa', they said, a maddening catch-all term usually deployed whenever anything goes wrong. Raising the issue at FIFA or CAF was also pointless. Yet when international teams came to South Africa they were always treated well. I was often tempted to serve them some of their own medicine but Molefi was adamant that we would roll out the red carpet for visiting squads irrespective of our opponent's behaviour when we visited their country.

In 2009 I returned once more to Nigeria with the under-20 national team to play another qualifier, this time for the upcoming World Cup. Our squad, a cheery gang of bright-eyed youngsters, not much more than girls who had never been out of their home towns let alone left the country, had no idea what they were in for. Worldly wise they were not.

We were met at Lagos airport by representatives of the Nigerian Football Federation. As usual we were sardines in a tin, crammed into a tiny bus with too few seats. And the driving? The word reckless doesn't cover it. How we never had a serious accident I will never know. Anyway, off we went into the jungle looking forward to settling in to our digs in some far-flung town and preparing for the game the following day.

What I came to realise after many visits to the country was that few Nigerian drivers used petrol stations to fill up their tanks. There was some issue (never fully explained to me) that people were unhappy about the government selling off petrol and oil overseas. Consequently locals sold fuel that they had seemingly siphoned off the main pipelines and sold it to drivers in small plastic containers. Even for someone who knew little about cars, I thought that the amount put into the tank wouldn't take us too far. It was not a joke. Every few miles we ran out of fuel and had to pull over where the driver would get out and whistle for someone to come out of the bush with a container of petrol. The transaction complete, off we would go once more—but only as far as the meagre top-up would allow.

This continued for hours on end, through the heat of the day and well into darkness. I was really scared I can tell you, as we were in thick jungle by this time and whenever we stopped, a posse of people would crowd around and inquisitively stare into the bus, probably wondering what planet we were from. I was trying to keep my composure for the sake of the wet-behind-the-ears players, but the girls must have been freaking out. Our kit manager lost his cool completely and threatened the driver that if he did not fill the petrol tank enough to get us to the final destination, there would be serious consequences. While, logically, we knew this was just a delay tactic to scare the young players and technical staff, it had the desired effect of stirring up our pre-match nerves. After an eight-hour nightmarish drive through the bush and being ogled at as though we were circus freaks, we finally arrived at our team hotel in pitch darkness.

As if that was the end of our nightmare. We were escorted to a dingy hotel—no lights, no water, no ceiling (!), nothing worked, cobwebs everywhere. The abandoned hotel had not been occupied for years. I asked the supposed hotel manager where we could get water for washing and to flush the toilets. He showed us some buckets and told us to go to the river (not even a hydrant this time). This abuse of my players was against all FIFA regulations for a World Cup qualification match, but what were we supposed to do? There was no match commissioner in sight and no one to complain to. The girls were terrified. Some of them must have thought that if this is international sport, you can keep it. And they hadn't even kicked a ball yet.

I later learned that the match commissioners, who rarely showed up to check on us, and who stayed in nice hotels, had little power to change the situation. We really were at the mercy of the Nigerian federation who would pull every trick in the book to unnerve us.

By the time we got 'settled in' to our cosy place in the country (around 2 a.m.), the players were starving and we all went looking for food of some kind. We were escorted to another dingy room for supper where some strange concoction was placed in front of us. Nobody could identify what was on the plate, so not many ate supper that night.

When travelling in Africa we usually insisted on half a chicken per person because at least it was food we recognised and not some unidentifiable bush meat. Sourcing nutritious food was a constant worry on these overseas trips. Once we were located near the beach, so I requested fish for dinner thinking that a little protein would be helpful and should be fairly safe. Each player was presented with a fish head with the eyes staring up at them. On another occasion, no breakfast was offered so we bought a stack of French loaves, warm and fresh, for the hungry players. They ate their fill, breaking off big pieces and savouring every bite. Not the ideal preparation for the game! Dodgy food was not only a hazard travelling in Africa. On a team visit to China, dog was listed on the menu and we had to politely decline.

Back to the abandoned hotel... Somehow, after fetching water from the river for toilets and morning ablutions, the players made it through the rest of the night. Next day was the match. As hardened as I had become over the years of African travel, I found it difficult to concentrate on this particular game because I had six heavily armed military types behind the bench casually swinging their automatic weapons, half the time pointing at us. The game was a walkover; we were thrashed.

So, defeated in more ways than one, we packed up all our stuff and prepared for the long drive through the bush back to the airport to fly home. The same minibus that brought us picked us up once again and turned left instead of right out of the hotel, which I thought a little curious. He drove straight onto a six-lane highway and within an hour we were at the airport. No eight-hour journey through the jungle, no running out of petrol, no buying fuel from indistinct characters in the bush, nothing. We'd been had.

On our return to South Africa, I once more complained to our officials but as usual Oliphant said that we were soft. 'That's Africa,' he said, which was by now becoming a euphemism for 'Stop complaining!'

Usually it was better to play the away game first so that foreign teams knew they had to play the return match in South Africa and perhaps would be a bit more accommodating—but that rule did not apply to Nigeria. They played by their own rules. On one occasion the Super Falcons came to Johannesburg for an Africa Women's Cup of Nations game and complained bitterly about the service in a lovely hotel we had arranged in Esselen Park, a venue which Banyana Banyana often used.

Incidentally, this venue will forever be remembered for the training session that ended with a sting in the tail. Someone disturbed a bees nest, which unleashed a swarm that attacked the players, especially those with gel in their hair. One player, Amina, had fifty-three bee stings, which Mama Dara had to extract.

Back to the Super Falcons... Lounging on the verandah like some gaggle of spoilt brats, the players and team officials sounded off about the accommodation to anyone who would listen and demanded they be moved to the more upmarket Milpark Holiday Inn. Then, because we took too long about moving them, they phoned the media to drop us right in it. SAFA complied and moved them to Milpark.

Travelling with broadly naive young women, many of whom had never been overseas, meant that we could be subject to, shall we say, unwelcome scrutiny from boys, foreign officials, con artists, and a swarm of random men with base intentions. For that reason we started travelling with our own team security: Frans Malatji, an ex-government security officer, and James Mofokeng or 'Weewee' as he was known.

Frans was a big, strapping man who made me and the girls feel safe in most situations. He took his job seriously and was always smartly dressed and kept good time; you could set your watch by him. But Weewee, a former *uMkhonto we Sizwe* ANC cadre with a serious drink problem, was forced upon the squad by SAFA president Olifant. At one time Olifant had been a teacher and James his pupil who had later fallen on hard times after leaving the ANC army. You get the picture.

On one trip to Nigeria Weewee accompanied the team. At that time everyone—both players and staff—was given a set of casual clothing for each day of the 'tour' branded by our sponsors, Adidas. After a few days I noticed that Weewee was wearing the same clothes every day. His routine on that trip was to accompany the team to the training field then go and lie down at the furthest end and go to sleep until it was time to head back to the accommodation. Some security. I spoke to the kit manager to follow up on Weewee's curious movements only to discover that when his kit bag was checked, there were no clothes inside, only alcohol.

On another occasion, in Kaduna State, we were preparing to leave the Handala Hotel for the airport but the management locked the gates and would not allow our bus to leave. On investigation it was found that Weewee owed the hotel's regular ladies of the night a significant amount of money for services rendered and they wanted to be paid. He had to forfeit his watch and I chipped in from the SAFA petty cash to get us out of the hotel compound and make our flight. SAFA funds to pay off hookers? How would I have explained that to the fastidious finance department?

Speaking of which, our SAFA finance department was a royal pain in the ass when it came to petty cash—every last cent had to be accounted for. If you've ever travelled through some of the less developed areas of the continent you will know how difficult it is to get something as simple as proof of purchase. How do you extract a receipt from a young boy selling blocks of ice from a cooler box? Ditto for bananas and fruit from a roadside gogo, never mind the airport bribes just to get the luggage loaded (US dollars only). No hard luck stories were accepted on my return. If I could not produce a receipt, I had to cover it out of my pocket.

Oddly enough, considering all the run-ins we had over the years, I came to terms with Weewee and all his quirks, and we are now good friends. Despite his, shall we say, lapses of concentration, he always stood up for me, especially when a man called Eddie du Plooy tagged along on our overseas trips as the SAFA head of delegation. Eddie was a rum bugger, which is a polite way to describe him given his predilections. I shall talk more about him later.

For the 2002 African Women's Championships we were based for about three weeks in an unusually nice hotel in a place called Oghara in Delta state, Nigeria. (When teams were in town for more than one game an effort had to be made!) We enjoyed pleasant rural surroundings and a quiet neighbourhood, the perfect environment in which to prepare for the matches ahead. The hotel was situated on a wide stretch of the River Ethiope. In fact it was so relaxing that some of the team got a little bored, which was probably a combination of being away from home and sheer anxiety to get on with the games. One day our team security, Frans, decided to venture out and explore the locality. He soon chanced upon an old sports club nearby that had been built by the British when they had occupied Nigeria many years before independence. It had a soccer field and a clubhouse with a well-used snooker table, dartboard and table tennis table. We checked with tournament coordinators and they agreed that we could use any of the facilities at the club.

Frans also made friends with some Afrikaners. This was more unusual than it sounds because I rarely saw another white whenever I travelled in Nigeria, except for our travelling physiotherapist Carin Fleishman. The South Africans were contract workers for a milling company, who often went on river picnics in small motorboats. They said they had discovered a small bay about fifteen minutes ride through dense jungle, where they had built a seating area. Just like home. After consultation with the relevant authorities we got permission for the team and technical staff to ride in a convoy of boats for the picnic upriver. It was great fun and turned into a great mental holiday for the Banyana Banyana girls.

Some of the technical team, which included Frans, our team psychologist and team doctor, suggested we explore the surrounding area, accompanied, of course, by two heavily armed soldiers who needed pangas to cut a path through the undergrowth. Real colonial era stuff. I was always up for a little adventure so tagged along.

As we made our way through the bush we came upon a small family in a clearing who were as surprised to see us as we were them. A woman was squatting down cutting up meat with a machete on the stump of a tree trunk. We ventured nearer. Suddenly the team doctor gave out a gasp and told us to turn back. She ran off towards the boats. We couldn't see why she had such a sudden change of heart but she had obviously seen something from which we should be shielded. We didn't stick around to find out, so we all ran after her towards the river. It was only as we arrived back at the picnic area that she revealed that the meat the woman was cutting up was human. They were cannibals.

Earlier I mentioned our occasional head of delegation called Eddie du Plooy and promised to get back to him. Eddie was a curious, jovial fellow, an ox of a man who was unmistakable because of his raucous laugh, and because he always wore a striped deerstalker hunting hat of the kind Sherlock Holmes popularised. I'm not sure what his heritage was but he could not speak any of the local black languages, preferring to speak Afrikaans with everybody, whether they understood him or not. When he first attended executive committee meetings in the 1990s he represented a region called Border, and was always complaining about something or other. There's one on every committee. Somebody above my pay grade decided that to shut him up he should be voted onto the NEC.

By this time whenever teams travelled abroad, one of the Exco members was appointed to travel with the team as head of delegation, even though they had no training for the job. It seemed to me that their appointment was a ruse to claim a rather handsome per-diem rate for doing next to nothing. They were supposed to mingle with their opposite number in whichever country we were travelling to, but once abroad they did as they pleased. The HOD was generally well-connected to the SAFA hierarchy. Eddie was no exception—he was a big buddy of Molefi Olifant. Say no more.

Whatever Eddie's political connections, he should never have been allowed anywhere near the women's national team. When I first heard he had been assigned to the squad I complained bitterly, but because he was 'protected' I had no chance of overturning the decision.

He was always smartly dressed and groomed (including the deerstalker), but sartorial elegance will only take you so far, especially when you've got a vocabulary like Eddie's. His favourite word was 'fok', which needs no more explanation. He would generally both start and finish a sentence with it, use it as a term of abuse or endearment, surprise or anger. He never censored his language in front of the girls in the team, which used to make me wince (I could be quite protective of the young ones).

When he wasn't 'fokking' his way through some diatribe or other, he was indulging his penchant for rum and Coke. Indeed, his day began with a double measure for breakfast. He would merely colour the rum with a drop of Coke and slug it back. If the waiter brought the wrong brand of rum, he would complain like only a thirsty ox can and demand another one. Apart from his formidable constitution with regards to alcohol, Eddie had an innate ability to attract a bevy of ladies wherever he went, which often put me in a compromising position.

There was one incident in Nigeria that illustrates his attitude to his role as head of delegation perfectly. After the whole squad, staff and Eddie had spent the day on the training field, we returned to the team hotel to find five ladies waiting at reception. Eddie uttered his usual expletive 'fok' from which I judged that these were his lady friends from the night before who had come back for more. He studiously ignored them and carried on upstairs with the rest of the team. Soon after, Eddie came to my room and said that due to a predicament in which he found himself (no doubt of his own making), I needed to come downstairs with him. As we walked down to the ladies of the night in reception he linked his arm in mine and proceeded to introduce me as his wife. They soon scurried off.

Continuing the sexual theme, I have never met a man so obsessed with his private parts. He was always bragging about his prowess. The flush of a typical Nigerian toilet tends to fill to a high water mark in the bowl, which would prompt Eddie to brag about how his privates had been dipping in the water as he sat on the john. He thought it was hugely amusing, but he would loudly relay these stories within earshot of the young players, and would embarrass me and the staff immensely. I reported his behaviour to my SAFA bosses many times but nobody listened. He was untouchable, and that was that.

On another trip, for no apparent reason, he decided that, after many years of travelling together, he disliked me after all. Maybe he had been tipped off by someone at the SAFA office that I took a dim view of his boorish behaviour. It came to a head, as these things do, after a number of drinks at a reception in the house of the South African ambassador in Kenya. He certainly picked his moment. Eddie became abusive to me, but luckily my friends Frans and Weewee the security guys disliked him immensely, and told him to back off or he would regret it. For some reason that incident never found its way into Eddie's head of delegation report on his return to SAFA.

After a few years, when his friends in high places moved on, my time with Eddie thankfully came to an end. He was also kicked off the NEC. After he left, having forgotten our little spat, on several occasions he had the cheek to phone me to scrounge some free match tickets.

11

FRANCE 98

As SAFA grew, so too did the number of contracted businesses that would pitch their services to the organisation, effectively bees around the footballing honeypot. One such was a man called Robin Ball, who was always trying to source work for his agency, Champions Tours, that sold travel packages for various tournaments.

In 1997 for the first time Bafana Bafana qualified for the following year's FIFA World Cup in France. I was keen to go to the tournament and watch the team play, but the perilous state of my finances would not allow it and, as self-appointed organiser of women's football, SAFA would not pay my passage. One day I was at the SAFA offices for a press conference when I bumped into Robin, a big bustling man who gave off an aura of nervous energy. I asked him what he was up to. He mentioned that he had

FRANCE 98

organised some tour groups to go to France for the World Cup.

Stupidly (in retrospect) I joked that if he needed a tour guide to let me know as I was desperate to go but had no funds. He immediately said 'Yes'. He knew I was an experienced traveller by this time and had some knowledge of France so I would have been useful, but there was something in his eagerness to sign me up on the spot that should have given me pause for thought. I thought, *Why was that so easy?*

I took advantage of the upcoming trip to treat my folks to their first ever overseas trip. My Dad hated flying so I was going to keep my plans secret until the last possible moment. They needed to apply for passports ahead of the trip so I made an excuse that he was going to neighbouring Swaziland to play golf. As the date for their flight loomed, Dara stepped in and rightfully said my parents can't be sent off unknowingly to Europe, so I told them that I had been planning for them to visit Wales to see some old friends and rediscover his roots in Brecon. Then it was on to Amsterdam to return to Mom's roots in Alkmaar.

Dad was apprehensive about the trip that was now only a few weeks away, but I was not taking no for an answer. He finally came around to the idea when we helped him visualise singing with a Welsh choir and having a few pints in the local. The plan was to meet my parents on arrival in Amsterdam from England, all I needed was for Robin to arrange my flight from France on the correct date.

Robin suggested that, before the departure of Champions Tours, all the tour guides and punters meet at his house for cheese and wine and a briefing. That all sounded very civilised; I went but not one participant showed up. Robin came up with some lame excuse for the no-shows but was adamant that we would meet them all before our departure. It never happened.

The first time the guides met the tour groups was at the airport check-in. And what a shock. The 150 people before me presented a strange demographic for passengers heading for the French Riviera. There were large groups of men—and a few women—who were all shebeen owners from Soweto, basically semi-legal tavern owners from the townships, tough businessmen and women who had been hardened by years in the trade. It turned out that they had all won an SAB (South African Breweries) prize of an all-expenses paid trip to the World Cup because they had sold the most beer. No sweat, Fran; this is not the time to panic.

To make matters more complicated, each group was flying on a different flight, some via cities in far-off places —no doubt to save on costs for Robin.

So now I had met the tour group, what about a travelling party list, a venue timetable... match tickets? Robin was still being coy about the arrangements. I asked him again, where is the delegation list? Where are we staying? Who is picking us up on arrival? Where is my petty cash? *Tickets*? He said he would bring it all to me before we boarded, and to hurry as we must check in the groups he had assembled. There was a lot of activity but not a lot was getting done. I noticed that everybody was turning to everybody else for guidance, and meeting equally guileless looks of confusion.

He then introduced me to one of the seven groups of about twenty-five smartly dressed travellers complete with their South African supporter scarves. I tried my best to look and sound like a tour leader by listing some of the great experiences we would have in *la belle France*. I was feeling a growing sense of unease as they all hung on my every word. The more they evidently placed their trust in me the less of a tour leader and more of a fraud I felt.

Then Robin grabbed me and said I must rather take a different party as they had already started checking in. Things were moving apace by this stage, what with the bags and passports and paraphernalia, so I rushed off to my new group, all the time asking Robin for the missing paperwork and travel itinerary. Nothing.

Suddenly we were all on the plane. I had the new group around me, not knowing who they were and them not knowing me. Clearly most of them had never flown before, so I was forever explaining the most basic functions of modern air travel—how to buckle up, use headphones, switch on the TV, open tray tables, order food, directions to the toilet. I'm sure some of them were not even in my party. Once everyone settled in for the long flight my thoughts turned to what on earth was going to happen on arrival.

Ten hours later, picture the scene... twenty-five eager shebeen owners dotted around their assorted luggage in the Nice Airport arrivals lounge looking for guidance from a white tour guide who had no more idea of where they were going than they did. I looked around in the faint hope that someone might come to meet us and lead us to our accommodation. Nothing. Perhaps Robin booked a bus that is now waiting for us outside. Please God, help me! Thank the Lord, there was a bus marked "Champions Tours".

'Where are we going, leader?' everyone asked. It was a difficult situation, but I had to be honest: 'I don't know.' Those three words nearly got me beaten up, well deserved given the circumstances. Luckily the bus driver had been briefed and off we went. We arrived at a smart but staid old *pension* on the *Promenade des Anglais*. Hungry and thirsty from the long journey, my group trooped in and immediately looked for a lounge, bar or dining room, but there were no common areas. Even though the travellers knew the prize only offered bed and breakfast accommodation, few had any spare cash for what I would have thought were quite important necessities—such as lunch and dinner.

They quickly formed a huddle and discussed how to capitalise on breakfast. They decided that they would eat as much sausage, eggs, bacon and toast to last the rest of the day and also take a *skaftini*, or takeaway box, for good measure. They asked the landlady where they could eat... now, if possible, as they were starving. She said that as there was no dining room in the *pension* a continental breakfast would be brought to the rooms in the morning. Stunned silence. I knew what a continental breakfast consisted of, but kept quiet. The landlady asked if they preferred tea or coffee in the morning, quickly making a note of their orders before leaving. I had no money. They had no money. There was no café or place to buy bread or any other staple. Disappointed, they drifted off to bed hungry. I braced myself for what I knew would be an insufficient breakfast for everyone.

Next morning each room was delivered a single warm croissant and a cup of tea or coffee. I soon had a riot on my hands. Where was the cooked breakfast? What about the *skaftini*? I had no option but to find a shop nearby and use my credit card to buy bread, cheese and ham to pacify the shebeen owners. I then traipsed out once more to find a phone box to call Robin Ball and read *him* the riot act. He didn't pick up. I imagined him looking at my name on his ringing cellphone and deciding it was a confrontation he could do without. But he would have to face me eventually.

What to do now? We had a few days to kill before the first match so I decided to take the group for a walk along the beach. Well, we were on the French Riviera, and it might be enough to keep them amused while I try to figure out how to occupy the rest of their time and also how to get hold of Robin and strangle him from 6,000 miles away.

As we were walking along the promenade I saw a colourful patch up ahead and as it got closer it transformed into the other tour group in their smart South African scarves who were initially given to me at OR Tambo. Now *they* wanted to kill me for abandoning them at the airport. They had flown on a later flight without a tour guide and without an airport pick-up, and somehow had made their way on foot to the beach where they had spent the night. There was no explanation I could offer that would pacify them.

In a spirit of *ubuntu* my group came to their rescue and invited them to pull in with us in our hotel, which they happily did either by sharing beds or sleeping on the floor. Predictably the landlady went berserk and called the police to have the second group evicted. I now had my hands full trying to explain in broken French how the fans had been let down and that their predicament was not of their own making. When my matric French deserted me, I resorted to outright begging. I must have reached her soft spot (it was in there somewhere) because with a Gallic shrug of the shoulders she finally gave in and allowed them stay.

I still couldn't get a call through to the missing Robin Ball. After a couple more days kicking our heels, it was still just me and a large group of hungry, irate shebeen owners on the French Riviera. I had spent all my personal money and the credit card was maxed out and we hadn't yet seen a match.

Then I was thrown a lifeline. One member of the group had the phone number of someone at SA Breweries back home so we called them from a call box and managed to convince them of our desperate situation and to transfer some money for food, which they did. Hunger satisfied, landlady appeased, and Fran calmed, we looked forward to Bafana Bafana's first match in Marseille against the host nation and one of the hot favourites, France. Massive game. Champions Tours and SA Breweries had finally got their act together and booked a train for all the tour groups to travel en masse to the match. As we reached the station the other five groups appeared, which ensured there was a happy reunion. Finally there were some good African vibes in the air.

Better still, someone from SAB had also arranged for stacks of Castle beer to be delivered to the station. Everyone loaded up a tray or two for the journey ahead and, not having had a whiff of alcohol for a week, the pre-match atmosphere improved by the minute. Of course the beer was warm but that did not stop anyone from glugging it down with gusto and getting merry.

When we arrived in Marseilles we saw that in anticipation of fan trouble the station was packed with French police armed to the nines. Our large extended group, some now well oiled, spilled off the train and headed for the toilets—which required a one-euro coin *à la Française* to gain entry. Which nobody had. The shebeen owners, to a man, their bladders full of their stock in trade, unzipped themselves and urinated onto the track like a wondrous railway fountain. The military, now pointing guns at a line of Africans relieving themselves probably wondered, *This was not the kind of crowd trouble we were expecting*.

Robin Ball finally got word to us to say that he was now in France, and promised to meet us at the stadium entrance with the tickets. As expected, the game had kicked off long before we saw any sign of him or the match tickets. Finally the big bustling man appeared and was immediately confronted by all concerned—I was at the front of the queue.

To top off a strange day, South Africa lost 3–0. Downcast, we returned to the waiting train which still had plenty of undrunk beer. Perhaps things weren't so bad after all. Despite a valiant effort, they didn't quite drink it all so they carried what was left back to the *pension* and opened a make-do shebeen in one of the rooms, selling Castle beer to the locals who were only too keen to try our South African brew. When the landlady discovered the speakeasy she once more did her Gallic nut.

To add to the chaotic nature of the trip, Robin Ball once again dropped me in it. He neglected to book my flight to Amsterdam in good time, which meant I would not be there for my folks' arrival. I had meticulously planned their first overseas trip but it was now unravelling before me.

Luckily I must have had a premonition that things would not go as planned because I had written a long note for Mom about what to do if I didn't show up. I just hoped they would follow it.

I landed the following day and caught the tram to their hotel. As I walked into the hotel, I saw my Dad sitting forlornly at the bar as only a South African in chilly Europe can. I had brought two six packs of Castle with me, which he was excited to share with the barman and brag about the finer points of South African beer.

12

HIGH PERFORMANCE

The year 2001 was a watershed for me in many respects. If someone had told me that I would be hired by the world body of football, meet my hero on his front porch, develop plans for a national performance centre for women's football, and take centre stage at a beauty pageant by the end of the year, I would have said they were either dreaming or needed to cut down on the cocktails.

I shall take the last of those unforeseen circumstances first.

Somewhat bizarrely, despite my sideways move to national teams manager, I was selected to be one of four icons at the Miss South Africa beauty pageant, one of TV's most watched events of the year. I was chosen for my involvement in women's football; the other three were top names from the corporate world. You may have guessed by now that frilly frocks are not my scene, but the organisers offered five-star accommodation for me and Dara, so I ditched my usual jeans and T-shirt and prepared to be pampered. My niece Leigh also managed to score three tickets to the event for herself, my sister Lynda and a friend. We could now make a party of it.

The idea on the night was that the icons would be trotted out to be introduced to the packed Sun City Superbowl while the beauty contestants were changing their outfits for the next segment of the show. The organisers informed me that the icons would be dressed in an exquisite outfit for which I had to be fitted at the offices of two of the top designers of that time: Marc and Michael. Unfortunately, after the show we would have to return the outfits, which cost thousands to make. For me this would be a one-off event so, in for a penny, I went full monty and ordered a ball gown to be made! After a number of fittings Marc and Michael created a full-length crimson dress with slim shoulder straps that was covered in Swarovski crystal. Everything was in place for a memorable occasion.

I couldn't wear high heels at the time because, after years of painful arthritis, I had to have two knee replacement ops, both of which were now in bad shape. So the day before we left for Sun City I bought a light pair of silver toe sandals with a thong between the big toe and second toe. It was a little flimsy but it was only for one night. What could go wrong?

Now I was ready and off we went. Dara and I were treated like royalty from the moment we were met at the Palace of the Lost City by suited butlers who showed us to our luxurious suite. Heaven.

On the Saturday afternoon we had a quick dress rehearsal with the stage manager to confirm our positions and arrange the best camera angles. As I was doing my thing, I realised that the strap around my heel was slipping. Simultaneously the sole shifted around and I began wobbling about on my already unsteady legs. A little unnerved, I made it through the rehearsal and went into make-up for the show ahead. I tried to tighten the heel strap as much as possible but it was already fixed on the last eyelet. There was nothing more to be done at such a late stage.

The afternoon sped by and soon the glamorous event was underway—packed auditorium, spotlights on, cameras rolling. It came to be my turn to be introduced to the packed crowd and TV audience of millions. I had spent the previous hour fiddling with the straps on the shoes, trying to get them to do what they were clearly not designed for—staying on the feet. I had a choice of walking barefoot or chancing the sandals. I would have looked strange coming on without shoes when my fellow icons had swanned on in their Christian Louboutin heels. But if my sandals slipped off, I was dead. I decided to chance it by not lifting my feet, but rather sliding like a penguin on ice. But in my case I wasn't cool because by now sweat was seeping through my make-up as I was introduced to the audience. *Lord please help me not fall and make a nana of myself in front of thousands of people.* Inside I prayed fervently and tried to force a smile.

I hardly remember the interview. After the longest five minutes of my life I slid off stage, doing my damnedest to remain upright. I had made it. Now I could relax. I threw the sandals in the bin and went barefoot to the after party which turned out to be one of the most memorable for Dara and me and the whole crowd. In fact, I shall take that back because I can't remember too much about it as I was so intent on celebrating not sliding into the audience at Miss South Africa.

The shoes were history, but the organisers allowed me to keep the dress. If I had known that beforehand I would have ordered something a little more practical. On my return home the gown was hung in the wardrobe where it hasn't moved to this day.

On my return from Utah, my plans to find a facility for women's football began to take shape. I had learned that women's soccer was a massive participation and spectator sport in the USA, helped by the fact that the US women's team have now been world champions four times (unlike the men's team who have been underachievers). Most little girls choose soccer as their team sport of choice, and many teenagers are scouted by colleges and universities. This combination of sporting excellence and academic ambition sounded like a great plan to me.

South Africa lagged behind this enlightened approach to girls' education. In fact some of our top players left school early to concentrate on their football. It wasn't only America that was forging ahead. In my travels overseas, I saw that many countries were ploughing investment into the future of the game by creating sporting academies. It got me thinking whether such a facility could be created in South Africa.

During my days as national coach it was apparent that, talented as they may have been, the players coming to camp were rarely match fit. Initially I knew little about their home situations, but my best guess was that their families were struggling with serious financial hardship, which had knock-on effects on their nutrition, mental health and access to sports facilities. Sometimes they would arrive already injured because they were running themselves into the ground playing for teams that had no medical oversight. Consequently two problems had to be tackled immediately: firstly, the players were not well nourished. In camp we would do our best to feed them up and get them fit for the duration of the training camp but then they returned home to the same old story. Secondly, the players were often not well educated. Schools in many townships were notoriously under-resourced and poorly managed, so the pupils rarely attained more than a basic level of education.

In 2003 I met an American friend of Kalamazoo Mokone who was involved with sports marketing company IMG and had connections with Tuks High Performance Centre in Pretoria. He invited me to come along and perhaps consider starting a girls' soccer project. I was already way ahead of him. It was the 'in' I needed.

The HPC was out of this world. A five star centre that catered for the needs of athletes' from different sporting codes, such as cricket, athletics, swimming and tennis. They had newly built blocks of accommodation, a communal canteen, a swimming pool and a medical treatment centre. There was also a block of enhanced living quarters where top-class athletes from overseas could be accommodated, including top teams from Europe that would come out to escape their cold winters. The place was so classy that the Argentinian men's football team stayed during the 2010 World Cup, Diego Maradona included.

As I walked around the HPC I knew that this was the environment in which my girls would thrive.

I firmed up my plans and approached the SAFA CEO and the women's committee with my proposal. SAFA agreed—as long as it didn't cost them anything and Fran Hilton-Smith did all the work. No change there.

As head of women's football, the HPC would be placed under my responsibility. I couldn't have been happier. Once I did the sums, I knew that the expense of the project was going to be an obstacle, so I applied to the National Lottery, which granted enough money to get the scheme off the ground. To further save costs our soccer players would have to share four to a room (rather than singles or sharing with one other).

HIGH PERFORMANCE

Now I had to source the girls for the first intake in January 2004.

I decided to focus on girls who were top class players and were also doing well at school, often despite difficult circumstances. I also considered their financial background. With assistance from my colleagues, we chose our first twenty-five girls.

The HPC was not only a sporting and educational facility, but also a home from home. Some girls had never been away from their mothers before so we required a housemother to oversee their pastoral needs. Josina Tellie, or Granny, as she was known, was taken on as the first housemother and remained in post for over a decade. Ria Ledwaba managed the centre for the first two years; Sheryl Botes was appointed as coach.

I believed that the High Performance Centre was key to nurturing a uniform approach to coaching that would transform our fortunes. Having one physical location for the women's national teams would also help us provide a more holistic programme of care. No less important was psychological evaluation and support for personal and psychological issues such as mental strengthening and sporting focus.

Finally, the education programme at the HPC was so important. Football required a keen understanding and a special kind of sporting intelligence to be able to read a game and communicate with teammates.

Now that I had a little support from SAFA, I was once again fired up at the potential. I made the arrangements at the university and did all the preparatory groundwork for the first intake of girls. Twenty-five players, mainly from underprivileged backgrounds, who could not have dreamed of such an opportunity, were the lucky guinea pigs for the programme that offered a 50:50 split between sport tuition and conventional education. They had their own school, medical centre and psychologist, regular nutritious food and, crucially, high expectations from the coaches. And it was all free. What a difference it made—to the team, to our overall performance, and to the girls' future prospects.

I was thrilled for the girls and their families, who could now see a future laid out before them. All we asked of them was to work hard and strive to reach their potential.

The first group of players came from as many different cultural backgrounds as there are in the rainbow nation: Zulu, Xhosa, Sotho, Tswana, Pedi, Afrikaner, etc., and it took a while for them to integrate. In some cases the clash of cultures accentuated their differences in traditions, languages and lifestyles, but generally speaking I was pleased to see the efforts the girls made to understand each other and 'cross the divide'. By this time there were not many white girls still playing outdoors because the outdoor game had largely moved to the townships where whites were not keen to go. Consequently many now played indoor football, which they perceived as offering better security. Nevertheless Janine van Wyk, Kylie-Ann Louw and Mandy de Araujo all made the cut for our first year's intake.

As an attempt at integration I asked the players to write a few sentences in each others' language. For instance, I asked Janine to write something in isiZulu while her opposite number wrote something in Afrikaans. Janine's mother called me to complain, 'Why must Janine write isiZulu?' I had to explain that I wasn't trying to indoctrinate her, but rather it was a long-term exercise in team building.

The excitement was palpable. There was no knowing at that early stage where a young player might go with talent, determination, professional guidance and plenty of sweat and application. The results soon bore fruit and justified all the effort to get the programme off the ground. For instance, Kylie-Ann Louw, a Banyana Banyana regular from 2005, was given an opportunity to study in the USA, and played in the Stephen F Austin State University team before moving into coaching. In 2012 she received her bachelors degree in kinesiology, followed by a masters in exercise science and human performance. She was voted the best player in the US collegiate league three years in a row. Academically strong, she won the Southland Conference Soccer Student Athlete of the Year award in 2011 and 2012 on top of many coaching awards from the Coaches Association of the USA. All thanks to football and, I like to think, helped along the way by the High Performance Centre.

Another success story was Nompumelelo Nyandeni, known to all as Mpumi, who I discovered by sheer chance. In 2001 I was invited by my friend Dilly to come to an out of the way place called Kwaggafontein, north of Pretoria. He managed a team called Detroit Ladies and wanted me to come scout one of his players. After driving for God-knows-how-long through the bush I finally arrived at a desolate spot where there was a rough sandy pitch on which two teams of players were warming up in readiness for a game. The match kicked off and I cast my eye over the talent. But instead of confirming that his player had star quality, there was another little player who caught my eye: fourteen-year-old Mpumi, a pretty girl with a perfectly round head and face and the loveliest smile. She was quite small for her age, at 1.63m, but this was no hindrance on the pitch as she was surprisingly skilful and technically sound with great vision and awareness of the game.

I told Dilly that the squad had no place for the player I had come to see but that I wanted Mpumi to come to the HPC selection camp. There was one small difficulty: she could not speak a word of English. Despite this drawback she made the cut for our first intake. Mpumi duly arrived at the academy and proved to be not only a terrific player but also a clever girl. I managed to attract the attention of a sponsor, Macsteel, who were keen to support boys and girls who were both bright in school and good at sport by paying for school fees, books and clothing. They immediately took her on. Hopefully the support would help her learn English so we could discuss team tactics!

On reflection, we were expecting a lot from one so young to adapt to such a strange environment; she was young and probably homesick, and at one time suffered distressing nightmares. The housemother Josina Tellie said that they would have to burn some traditional herbs called *mpepe* to rid the bad spirits and help her settle down.

Whatever Granny did worked. Within a year Mpumi had turned around her prospects and was one of four players invited to Arsenal FC in London for trials. As she was still underage I had to go and ask her mother, a domestic worker, if she could go overseas. The mother was fearful of losing her daughter but finally gave approval when I assured her that I would take good care of her. The Arsenal manager said Mpumi was her first choice of the four players I brought, but she was a year too young even for their junior intake.

Later she was signed by a Russian team called WFC Rossiyanka that played in the UEFA Champions League, reaching the quarter finals. That was a big deal for a young girl from Kwaggafontein. Coming from Africa it was always difficult for our players to adapt to the European climate, more so in Russia where temperatures often drop below zero. Mpumi said that she didn't know what to do with her hands and feet during games as they were mostly numb, and on top of that she had to play in shorts. Those African legs must have suffered!

By the time she left South Africa she had learned English, but none of her new Russian team mates spoke the language that she was so diligent in learning. She later told me that she got by on hand signals. Then the club signed an English speaker who said she would teach Mpumi Russian if she returned the favour and taught her English. She soon became fluent in Russian, which impressed the locals no end. I was always worried for her welfare, especially knowing she would feel the bitter cold, but she stuck it out for four years, 2010–2014.

When Mpumi finally returned home, a big portrait of her was put up in the clubhouse that honoured both her sporting contribution and for being an ambassador for South African football. She also served Banyana Banyana with aplomb, winning 149 caps for her country and scoring thirty-nine goals. In 2009 she was one of SAFA's Players of the Year and the SASOL Player of the Year and top goalscorer at the SASOL championships in 2009 and 2010. In 2009, 2010 and 2012 she was a nominee for the continent-wide CAF Player of the Year. She plays for the JVW team in 2021, and still looks so young.

She wasn't the only player whose life was transformed by attending the centre of excellence. Another time, after finishing her matric year, one of the girls wrote such a lovely letter explaining how when she arrived at HPC she came with no shoes and only the clothes on her back and one of the other girls gave her a spare cellphone and another gave her a pair of trainers, and now she was going to university. Who knows what that university education will lead to.

The first Indian player at the HPC and the first to play for Banyana Banyana was Robyn Moodaly, who progressed to be a top-class player. After completing her matric she earned a scholarship and university contract in the USA.

This project of mine was beginning to change girls' lives and give them an opportunity to study, which for many girls from deprived homes would never have been an option. It made me especially happy when players took their opportunities and ran with them. I was learning that a little encouragement often led to even more auspicious outcomes.

Some want to put something back into the game, which is how I see the women's game progressing in the years to come. So it was that in later years a project designed by Janine van Wyk and Banyana Banyana manager Lauren Duncan turned into the biggest schoolgirls' league in South Africa. Known as JVW, I predict that the league will become a role model project for other sports and for other countries in Africa.

While ex-players mentored the future stars of women's football, I made it my business to develop women coaches, for which I sourced funding from FIFA. I am proud to say that I mentored twenty-seven women who attained their CAF A licence—more than any other country in Africa—and all our national teams are coached by women. As I write, Desiree Ellis is Banyana Banyana coach, Simphiwe Dludlu is the under-17 coach (leading the team to two World Cups) and Jabulile Baloyi coaches the under-20s. Sheryl Botes has been in the HPC for years and also coached the under-20 women's national team, while Anna Monate coached at the HPC in the national team, and in China. Others have also done well.

Progress was not only made out on the field of play. Running a programme like the HPC also required a competent backroom team that could organise the academic and sporting curricula. As HPC manager for a number of years, Ria Ledwaba was responsible for the overall running of the centre. Meanwhile Josina Tellie, Granny, had an important role when caring for teenagers, and probably the person with the heaviest workload, what with having to look after the needs, desires and dreams of twenty-five young girls. She was taken on in 2002 and remained a constant fixture until her retirement in 2018. Granny made a big difference in many girls' lives.

HIGH PERFORMANCE

By now I was used to women's football being the poor cousin of the sport, and so it proved when it came to securing funding for the programme. Initially the Lotto sponsored the High Performance Centre, before handing it over to the SAFA Legacy Trust, but it became too costly for them to support us long-term. Women's football attracted a few corporate sponsors along the way, but not enough to make a significant difference. Sanlam Building Society was first on board when they sponsored the Halala Cup in 2002 and later the Sanlam league in the 2002–3 season. After SAFA were slow to pay out prize money (not an unusual occurrence) and teams contacted Sanlam headquarters to complain, the company withdrew its support. Very sad. This also happened when ABSA came on board. We had to wait a while longer before SAFA signed a Bafana Bafana deal with Vodacom and threw in women's football as part of the package.

I was the technical advisor and overseer of the project from its inception until my retirement, which was a full-time job in its own right, but of course I never received a cent for my efforts over the seventeen years.

That first intake took an age to arrange. And, of course, the selection process had to be repeated every year, which included trials, aptitude tests and interviews. We had taken on a huge, exhausting project—that was when everything worked smoothly. If players caused a problem at the school or in the accommodation or had to be picked up from the airport after missing the official transport or had boyfriend issues, I was called in on my own time. I also had to deal with parents who had to be placated and reassured. Then there were the neverending meetings and reports to be written. Let's not go there.

Despite all this extra time and effort, my involvement with the HPC was a joy. There were many great moments when players achieved great things at school, made the national teams or entered university.

It saddens me that SAFA allowed the numbers of HPC players to drop to thirteen—the intake in 2019 was only three, in 2020 it was zero. The corona virus pandemic meant that only a handful of students came in to complete their final year of school in 2020 (including head girl Shakira O'Malley who obtained five distinctions in matric and won a university scholarship in the USA), but hopefully this situation will improve and the HPC will bounce back better than before.

Anyway, back to my day job as national teams manager.

In 2002 Banyana was one of fourteen teams invited to the first ever Confederation of Southern African Football Associations (COSAFA) tournament in Zimbabwe. Palacios moved aside (he really only acted as a stopgap for the Utah tour), allowing Bafana Bafana coach Shakes Mashaba and assistant Neil Tovey to lead the team. We beat Zimbabwe in a heated final despite being stoned on our way into the stadium. We have since won the tournament another six times.

In 2002, for reasons known only to himself, Molefi Olifant gave the coaching job to ex-player Gregory Mashilo. I was devastated. He had clearly been appointed as the new broom and told to clean up, an instruction which he interpreted by dropping ten of our best players, including Maude Khumalo, Hilda Lekalakala, Sibongile Khumalo, and our long-standing captain, Desiree Ellis. We were invited to play China 2003----   I was still the Team Manager.

Mashilo's appointment as women's coach was a disaster. In 2003, despite my protestations that they were way out of our league, he agreed to two friendlies against China *in* China. He was stubbornly insistent that we could do well and that the experience would imbue the team with confidence. On the contrary, it was a case of too much hope over too little experience. We suffered two

HIGH PERFORMANCE

embarrassing losses—13–0 and 9–0—which demoralised the girls and showed anyone who cared to notice that not only was the new squad not up to the task of matching one of the world's premier sides, neither was the new coach. It almost beggars belief to say it now but the security guy Weewee got so angry during the first thrashing that he took over coaching duties in the second half. Augusto Palacios was even brought in to assist but could not improve the situation. Somehow I ended up getting the blame. Mashilo bungled along for three underwhelming years until Banyana Banyana were humiliated at home in the 2004 African Women's Championship, losing all three group stage games to Ghana, Zimbabwe and Ethiopia. He left in disgrace. After the tournament Olifant came to me and admitted that they had made a big mistake replacing me with Mashilo. Too late for that.

Meanwhile, in 2004, once again South African football was trying to make a name for itself on the world stage. After the devastating disappointment of losing out to Germany in the bid to host the 2006 World Cup, SAFA put together a new bid to host the next one, in 2010.

The winning country would be announced once more with great pomp and ceremony at an event in Zürich. Even ailing Nelson Mandela, who was clearly in no fit state to attend, was flown to the final draw at FIFA headquarters.

Dara and I needed to surround ourselves with other hopeful football fans on the night of the announcement, this time at a packed function at Vodaworld. There were thousands of people having a great time, partying away merrily as if we had already won the vote.

In a re-run of the announcement four years earlier, FIFA President Sepp Blatter stepped onto the stage holding the envelope with the winner's name. There was an eerie silence in the room around us, one strangely charged with hope and anticipation as no one dared breathe. Blatter opened the envelope.

'The 2010 FIFA World Cup will be organised by...'

Then he pulled the card from the envelope. Two words were written on it: "South Africa".

I have never experienced such jubilation and excitement in my life. People went crazy. Everyone was hugging each other, strangers embraced strangers, tears flowed, wall to wall smiles, and wide-eyed expressions of shock, hardly believing that our moment had come.

Outside on the streets the country seemed immediately buoyed on a wave of euphoria. Somehow all the social, political and economic problems we faced in South Africa were diminished by this victory. All anyone could talk about was hosting the World Cup six years hence. Everyone I talked to—both inside and outside football— were so proud that our country would be the first on the continent to host the World Cup. We couldn't wait to welcome the world. If we could have bottled that feeling of optimism it could have sustained us for years to come.

In 2005 Augustine Makalakalane was appointed coach and the results improved until Banyana Banyana failed to qualify for the World Cup; then some players accused him of sexual harassment and homophobia, and his contract was not renewed. His assistant Joseph Mkhonza took over.

Meanwhile as teams manager I was responsible not only for many aspects of all three teams' sporting prowess but also their well-being and morale. After recent defeats and disappointments, I decided a morale boost was what we all needed, and I knew just the man to turn to.

I have read other people's accounts of meeting Nelson Mandela and the indescribable aura that he projected. Similarly, now that I have experienced it, I cannot really explain the spirit of goodness that he exuded. The man was feared by many white South Africans during apartheid while he endured twenty-seven years of confinement in the name of democracy, yet went on to become one of the great political and humanitarian role models of our time. At one stage he was regarded as the most trusted man in the world. I *had* to bring the players to meet him.

Whenever Banyana Banyana were preparing for a tournament I wrote a polite letter to the president's office requesting that the senior women's team come and meet Madiba. He had long been retired from politics and I figured he might find an hour to support the team, as he had done for Bafana Bafana. No luck. In 2006 I tried again prior to leaving for the All Africa Games in Nigeria and received a letter from his PA to say he was resting in Mozambique with his wife Graça Machel and was not seeing anyone. However, as luck would have it, Madiba suddenly came back to Johannesburg. Soon after, Dara was invited to meet him with her boss, the chairman of Kaizer Chiefs, Kaizer Motaung. Needless to say I was green with envy. Kaizer and Madiba were long-time friends, Madiba having officially opened the Kaizer Chiefs soccer village. After the meeting Dara approached Madiba's personal assistant, Zelda la Grange, and told her how Banyana Banyana and myself had been trying so long to get an 'audience' with the great man, while Bafana had met him on a number of occasions.

Soon after, I got a call to say the meeting was on. Amazement all round. Thanks Dara, you made my dreams come true again!

A few months after performing for him at the president's residence in Pretoria, one sunny day we pulled up in the team bus outside the Nelson Mandela Foundation in Houghton, Johannesburg. Inside the bus were around twenty players and eight officials all with dry mouths and hearts pumping. The excitement was palpable. We were ushered onto the sweeping veranda of his beautiful home complete with grand pillars. We all gathered around the huge front door and waited apprehensively for him to emerge from the house. Suddenly the door swung open and the man himself appeared, supporting himself with a chrome-handled walking stick. His aide Zelda la Grange took the weight of his other arm. Bodyguards kept their distance. As usual he was wearing one of his colourful shirts that had become synonymous with his distinctive sartorial style. (One of his shirt designers was a man called Sonwabile and I later got him to make me some shirts.) But more than the loud shirt, the first thing we all noticed was the infectious Mandela smile—his eyes, mouth, even the wrinkles on his face seemed to smile. We were all in awe.

Rather than treating the meeting as a chore, the first words he uttered were, 'Thank you all for taking the time to come and visit me,' as if we were doing *him* a favour. 'It is so wonderful of you to come.' That was the humble man he was. Thanking *us* for the honour.

From the small stage of the presidential residence I had felt a rush of Madiba magic. Now, once again I was struck by his aura, something I had never felt so powerfully from another human being. I gingerly edged forward to greet him and hand him one of the black caps I had designed with "Banyana Banyana" embroidered in colourful cotton. He accepted it as if it were a valuable gift and placed it firmly on his head. He smiled, I smiled, we all smiled. Someone took a photograph. I was finished.

The girls were asked to form a single line where he took the time to greet each one individually and ask a personal question or two. Some would not have been born when Mandela was released from prison in 1990 nor when he became the first democratically elected president. Despite that, the awestruck girls felt his presence which made them shy and inclined to speak softly to the old man. He was by now hard of hearing so the girls were told to speak up.

Janine van Wyk was one of the few white players, unmistakeable with her dyed blonde hair. When she greeted Madiba in her heavy accent, without missing a beat he replied in Afrikaans, '*Hoe gaan dit?*' ('How are you?'). '*Gaan jy die toernooi in Nigerië wen?*' ('Are you going to win the tournament in Nigeria?') He had mastered the language of his persecutors in prison so he could communicate better with his jailers. In Afrikaans Janine replied that they would try their best. He giggled and broke into a broad smile.

Madiba then asked Keneilwe Mathibela what she had been up to and she replied that she had just been appointed team vice-captain and he congratulated her profusely and wished her well in Nigeria in her new role. Patiently he made his way down the line, holding the girls' hands in some cases and giving his full concentration to each person that allowed them an equal chance to chat. He seemed to have an original, kind word for everyone.

Later I asked Portia Modise about her conversation with him. Still in awe from the meeting, she said she was so starstruck she could not remember a thing he had said. Notwithstanding the occasional memory lapse, everybody came away with a personal memory of their time with the living legend. It would be something they could tell their grandchildren.

Ninety minutes after arriving, Madiba, still wearing the Banyana Banyana cap, was ready to return to the house. I bade him farewell and told him that we would do our best for him and the country and we hoped to be inspired by meeting him. No matter what would transpire at the tournament, we certainly were inspired. We all waved goodbye and Zelda led him slowly back into the house. The door closed. A memory captured in time forever.

During the 'audience', Zelda never left his side. She acted as both a reassuring presence to him and a gentle signal to visitors not to get too close. It always amazed me how he depended on her, a white Afrikaner woman, when his harshest prison jailers had been Afrikaners. He had met her when he came to the presidential office to take up his duties of state following the 1994 general election. Zelda had been an office typist/clerk. They clearly 'clicked' because she soon rose up the ranks. Later she would become more than just a member of staff. After Mandela left office in 1999 she assumed the role of secretary, confidante, aide-de-camp, spokesperson and almost constant travelling companion. She has joked since that she was his 'honorary granddaughter'. She remained at his side until his death in 2013. An amazing story; an amazing woman.

Nelson Mandela took centre stage once more a couple of years later. Six years after winning the bid to host the tournament, on 11 June 2010 in Pretoria, South Africa played the opening World Cup game against Mexico. The whole country was glued to their TVs and radios. The utter and complete joy of seeing Siphiwe Tshabalala score a sizzling shot from outside the 18-yard box into the top right-hand corner of the net was a moment that will stay with me forever. The country erupted.

With stadiums packed with fans from thirty-two nations, and each game celebrated in township shebeens and suburban bars—and the country's crime rate unexpectedly plummeting—South Africa felt like a different country. The 1995 Rugby World Cup was undoubtedly a watershed moment for the country, but this felt different—soccer was the *people's* sport; it was *my* sport.

A month later, I remember sitting in the stands for the Netherlands v Spain final when Madiba came onto the field with his wife Graça Machel. Now a frail man of ninety-two, he arrived on a golf cart and wearing an *ushanka*, or Russian fur hat, and thick black coat. The spectators went wild. He had brought the World Cup tournament home, and now the fans could show their gratitude.

13

JOIN FIFA, SEE THE WORLD

Returning to my watershed year of 2001, the third unexpected invitation of that year was something that turbo-charged my involvement in football and gave me new ways to not only improve the standing of the South African women's teams, but also the women's game around the world. FIFA came into my life.

Out of the blue I was contacted by a Swiss national called Tatjana Haenni from FIFA's Zürich headquarters, who said she was in charge of women's football. She asked me where I had sprung from and how the South African national team had risen so fast to second-place ranking in Africa. She asked me to send her a précis of my achievements in football, which I did.

Subsequently it emerged that FIFA were hoping to grow the sport in Africa, especially the women's game, and were looking for likely ambassadors on the continent. They didn't need to ask me twice. That short phone call led to me being appointed to the FIFA Technical Study Group (TSG) for the first under-20 Women's World Championship in Canada in 2002. God is great!

Even though the offer to join FIFA was somewhat random, I accepted it as a great reward for my years of hard work. Perhaps all those days organising games from the back of my car on either cold and wintery or hot and sweaty days had been worth it after all.

The study group was commissioned to write technical reports for FIFA competitions to analyse how the game was progressing through match-by-match analysis, detailed stats and honest appraisals of each team's performance. Essentially, FIFA wanted to pay me to go to the World Cup and write reports on the games. That I can do.

Three cities hosted the tournament in Canada: Edmonton, Vancouver and Victoria. I was lucky to be based in the last of these and reported on the games held at the Centennial Stadium. What a tremendous experience. I was the new kid on the block, but had two local ladies assisting me, and we were all eager to make a good impression.

FIFA provided us with expensive laptops so we could make notes at the stadium as the games progressed. However, my laptop did not come with a case so I packed it in a large carry bag we shared between us. One of the assistants decided to pack our water bottles in with the laptop. After one match we packed up to head home when I noticed to my horror one of the bottles had leaked. I opened the laptop, but it was soaked and failed to fire up. I was hysterical as I did not have another one and there was no one to help me in my predicament. I phoned home in a panic and Dara told me to blow it dry with a hairdryer. I sat for half the night pointing the hairdryer at the laptop praying it would come back to life. It did, early next morning. But I still had to write my match report and submit it. I had phoned my FIFA boss Tatjana to tell her of my dilemma but she was not interested in lame excuses. She just wanted the report. The next day I had another match; to say I was tired would be an understatement.

I so loved Victoria that when FIFA sent me to Canada for the 2015 Women's World Cup, I took Dara. Metro Gerela (the coach I'd met at that dodgy Sardinian tournament all those years earlier) booked us a float plane to fly from the Canadian mainland to Victoria. It confirmed to me that it was one of the most beautiful places I had ever visited. The bay, the islands, the houseboats, the little commuter planes, and the small vessels called pickle boats that took passengers around the little coves and inlets... so beautiful. For most of my subsequent FIFA trips to the World Cups around the globe I travelled with Dara because she only had to pay her own airfare to join me.

The relationship with FIFA worked for both parties: the powers that be at FIFA headquarters seemed impressed both with my work and also my struggles against seemingly insurmountable odds as a white South African fighting for women's football in a predominantly male sport; on the other side of the equation, I got to see the world following the sport I loved.

In 2003 there was talk that I may be asked to conduct an instructor's course somewhere in the world. I wondered where that might be. One of the giants of the game? USA? Norway? Canada (again)?

No... the Islamic Republic of Iran.

When I got over the shock, I told my parents about the offer. They both said 'No' on the spot. It was far too dangerous, they claimed. The country was under strict Islamic law and there were few civil rights for women and children, so how was a female liberal-minded gay biker rock musician going to fit in?

I pondered long and hard over the decision. I knew I had been chosen because FIFA viewed me as someone who would relish going to risky places. (How wrong can you be?) They probably thought that if I had succeeded in South Africa—and survived Nigeria—I could manage anywhere. Not quite. I was worried about the offer to visit Iran, there was no doubt about it, but I was also worried that if I refused I may not get a second chance. With more than a hint of trepidation, and several stiff whisky and Cokes, I accepted the offer. In for a penny.

What an experience.

Before I left, Iran's head of women's football wrote to remind me of the country's strict dress code and said that I had to wear a long formless jacket and headscarf at all times. This was non negotiable and I would likely be locked up by the police if I did not comply. I flew off to Iran with nerves and butterflies fighting for space in my stomach. Everyone on the plane was dressed more casually than I had expected and women had their hair uncovered, which surprised me. However, as we approached Iranian airspace, the female passengers started covering their heads. I did the same. At Tehran airport I retrieved my luggage and headed for the arrivals lounge. I was soon engulfed by that awful feeling of loneliness you get when all the other passengers are met by relatives and friends and then disappear out the exit doors. Finally I was standing on my own in a new brown formless jacket and brown scarf. No one in sight. Now I was scared. I had no phone, and no one to call even if I did. Should I take a taxi? But I had no local currency. And I didn't even know where I was staying. Oh, Lord.

After what seemed like an eternity I saw three black apparitions up ahead. I headed towards the burkas and could discern that they were three women behind the veils. I asked if they were from the women's football division. Yes. I wanted to hug them. I asked why they had not come forward to find me as I had been waiting ages and there was not another soul around. They said that they were looking for a black woman as they had been told the instructor was coming from Africa!

Next day we met at a sports centre to begin the course. I entered the room to find about thirty women covered from head to toe in long black robes and black headscarves. We then had to sit through interminable speeches—by men, of course—to the cowering, silent ladies. The atmosphere was tense with anticipation. What did this foreign instructor have in mind? When are these men going to shut up? It was one of the strangest pep talks I have ever witnessed.

Finally we were all led off to a gymnasium with high windows and a tall door, to prevent scrutiny from outsiders. Heaven forbid someone should catch sight of a woman! As if that wasn't enough, the men then locked us in the gym. I was in a frenzy by this stage. Then something happened I will never forget. Once the doors were double-locked from the inside, the ladies ripped off their long black jackets and scarves and veils and started laughing and giggling and talking at a rate of knots like children released for the summer holidays. They changed into shorts and jerseys and trainers and were soon ready to play indoor football like any other national team. In an instant they had transformed from faceless, formless beings into, well, beautiful women.

And these women were surprisingly good players because it was one of the few sports they were allowed to play, as long as they were covered up and kept out of the sight of men. We played enthusiastically for about two hours before our time was up. Before the men came to release us from the gym, I asked to take a photograph—some of the younger girls preferred to wear their veils, but the older ones were happy to go without. Two older ladies in particular explained that they had played during the previous regime under the Shah. One had been the captain of the women's national team when they were allowed to play outdoor football. I noted the bitterness in her voice when she explained how her life had changed now that she had to live under stringent Islamic restrictions. She told me that when the women were at home with their family, husbands and children, they could take off the veil, but everywhere else it had to be worn. Only face and hands may be seen in public; non adherence could be punished by up to ten years' imprisonment.

Women, she explained, were not equal under Iran's constitution, which strictly followed Sharia Law. In fact the law treated them as half a man, they inherited half what a man would, and compensation for the death of a woman was half of a man's. I was coming to realise that something as simple as playing a team sport like football was a major challenge for these women. My fear and apprehension was turning to admiration and a growing sense of sisterhood. As they reluctantly put on their regalia the mood sobered up and they became quiet and docile once again. We knocked on the door and they let us out into the man's world.

The big game in Iran at the time was indoor football but women were not allowed to attend, even as spectators. Three of the women took advantage of a FIFA official's presence to ask if they could watch a big indoor men's game. They said to me, 'If you ask our president while he is talking to the FIFA official, he is more likely to agree that you can watch the game as a FIFA delegate.'

They also wanted me to tell them that I would prefer to have some local women with me for 'protection'. None of them even came up to my shoulder, so how they were proposing to provide protection was a mystery.

Anyway, we went to the game, a local derby clash. I wasn't prepared for what was to come, and lived to regret it. I walked into the indoor stadium with 20,000 swaggering, baying spectators already worked up to fever pitch. Of course when they saw four women in the stadium they started performing like a bunch of frustrated zoo animals. We were subject to a dreadful display of incontinent male behaviour, the rudest gestures and the foulest language with exaggerated spitting. Luckily we were in a fenced-off area, but even so it was unpleasant to say the least. The three ladies who accompanied me were too thrilled to be watching a game to worry about the leering macho display.

Afterwards, the players pushed their luck once more when they talked me into asking the authorities if the women could play outside for a session—rather the request come from me, they said. The authorities (the men) agreed, even though women had not been allowed to play outside since the overthrow of the Shah in 1979. A field was designated for a ladies' game but no men were allowed. Even so, the players had to cover up, which meant no skin other than face and hands should be on display. Unfortunately FIFA had sent thick black Adidas tracksuits intended for the European winter, which the ladies had to wear to cover their legs. I had no choice but to keep on my long jacket and veil. All this in 45 degrees Celcius.

The ladies played for two hours, but even with that terrible heat they were reluctant to stop because they knew this was probably the only time they would be able to play on a grass pitch. For many of them it was. It was not until 2018, sixteen years later, that women were allowed to play outdoor football—with the help of some FIFA intervention.

My extraordinary week ended with a meeting at a restaurant where officials sat on the ground sharing food from a low table. Another time the players held a picnic for me in a forest. One of the coaches brought a long Persian carpet from home that she laid out on the forest floor where we snacked on cakes and juice and had a great time. I still treasure the Persian carpet they gave me as a going-home gift.

Far from the forbidding trip I had envisaged before I had set foot in Iran, I returned home enlightened, having experienced something very special.

I wonder now if the trip to Iran was a FIFA test, and that since I had come through the instructors' course unscathed, I deserved an easier posting for my next mission. Next stop: the island paradise of Vanuatu in the South Pacific. From the ridiculous to the sublime.

I was clearly doing something right because later they sent me to Trinidad and Tobago. I will never forget snorkelling on the beautiful reefs amongst dazzling tropical fish. This trip was also memorable because the course co-leader was my good friend and England coach Hope Powell. She came with a CV crammed with experience: after playing in four FA Women's Cup finals, she became the first full-time England coach and led the nation to four World Cup tournaments. She was also the first woman to achieve the UEFA Pro Licence. Later she helped develop a coach mentoring scheme at England's version of my High Performance Centre, at Loughborough University. In many ways she was a role model for female players, coaches and administrators. I could now see first hand what a knowledgeable instructor she was and I learned so much from her, for which she deserves much credit.

Years later the under-17s qualified for the World Cup in Trinidad and Tobago and I quickly wrote to my FIFA boss Tatjana and requested that the South African team be based in Tobago. Voilà, another month in paradise, and this time I could enjoy it with the whole national team. Some people call it work.

I was also sent to Thailand to lead a coaching course with the future Banyana Banyana coach Vera Pauw. I knew I had landed in a different culture when I went to the bar for a Coca-Cola and the waitress approached on her knees to serve me. The trip was unforgettable because before the course had begun I tripped and bashed my lip on a step. Vera had to cover my face with make-up every day, a rare but necessary intervention.

On another occasion, in 2003, I was in Washington DC as part of the women's study group for the World Cup. Shortly after my arrival I was informed that a tornado was about to hit town. Well they got that right. On my return to the hotel after a match, the guests were told to go to their rooms and prepare for the storm. Basically, batten down the hatches. Soon the whole building was shaking as I lay huddled on the floor watching the approaching storm on the TV news. My fear was interrupted by a telephone call. It was Tatjana who wanted her match report. I tried to explain that there was no network and I could not fax the report because the whole city was holding on for dear life. She was not buying it. I had to crawl out of my safe space and find the general coordinator of the World Cup to explain my predicament.

My time with FIFA led to me being taken on as an instructor at the Confederation of African Football (CAF) in 2005. I conducted many coaching courses for them, which usually took place in Ethiopia before they built a centre to honour the then CAF president from Cameroon, Issa Hayatou, so we had to traipse off to a relatively primitive camp in his home country. Cameroon was hot as hell and when the sun wasn't blistering it always seemed to be raining which, I suppose, took the edge off the tremendous heat. I guess that's a jungle for you.

The camp was located outside Yaoundé, a nightmarish two-hour road trip from the airport on a narrow road racing against endless huge logging trucks that hurtled along, which reminded me of my Nigerian journeys. I saw my life flashing before me more than once.

The venue itself had few creature comforts, and lacked such necessities as a tuck shop or TV reception or even a kettle in the room. There was a limited breakfast and nothing offered in between a basic lunch and dinner. The coir beds were like slabs of concrete. I had to pile up two or three mattresses to even attempt any sleep. And at the end of the day's instructing I could look forward to an African shower—the drippy, trickling kind. Clearly I was paying my dues for the relative luxury in the Caribbean.

As national teams manager I had to take on many logistical challenges that go with keeping three squads on the road. For instance, it was a constant struggle to get decent kit for all the teams—and to prevent it disappearing. As late as 2018 all three women's teams were sharing one set of boots—and then they were lent to the boys under-17 team who were also ill-shod. More embarrassingly, in the early days we were given old Bafana kit with the men's names on the back!

No matter how much I complained for more kit every year, no one took any notice. I was dismissed with, 'The budget has run out', 'The budget cannot accommodate'. Nobody gave a damn. If I was not present at a sponsor's meeting, the predicament of the HPC would not even be raised. So I spent my life stealing from Peter to pay Paul to get the twenty-five girls kit, boots and trainers. This included donating my own clothing and footwear so they would have some casual wear, or getting the girls invited to events where I knew they would be offered a T-shirt. If I ran a big course for FIFA or the Government I would often order a second set of T-shirts, tracksuits or boots and trainers for my HPC girls.

These may sound like desperate measures to acquire sports gear, but when some of the girls arrived at camp with nothing more than the clothes on their backs every piece of kit counted.

Even when the girls were entitled to their own kit we had to fight for it. The deal was that players were given their kit, tracksuits, boots and trainers for each camp they attended and at the end of training had to return it. Then at the end of each year the players—both men and women—were given all the kit they had worn that season. It seemed a small way of saying 'thank you' to the players, but we always had a battle with the SAFA head honchos and the kit room because they would never want to hand it over. The players often had to give one of their playing jerseys—with their names on the back—to the national executive committee. What did they plan to do with it? Members of the NEC were already receiving huge bags packed full of clothes and shoes every year, but not the girls.

At one time the petroleum giant SASOL only sponsored the under-23 men's team that played in the Olympics, but that was about to change. Our luck turned when, around 2009, Nolitha Fakude was appointed as a director of SASOL and she decided the company should sponsor the women's team instead. Banyana Banyana were in business. The energy company sponsored the yearly regional women's leagues in all fifty-three regions, culminating in the annual national club championships. Separately they also sponsored Banyana Banyana internationals against top opposition such as the USA, Sweden and the Netherlands. SASOL's support helped the team qualify for two Olympics, and the big one was yet to come. I will be forever grateful to Nolitha for changing the fortunes of Banyana and the women's league, and for treating the players with the respect they deserved.

With a committed sponsor on board, it was time to shout about it—or at least sing about it. At one of our regular SASOL meetings I suggested we compose a song for both the women's league and Banyana Banyana, something to get the fans excited. They thought it was a great idea. I immediately contacted my old musical buddy Leon Erasmus who was then running a recording studio in Newtown, Johannesburg. He was delighted to come on board and we spent many happy hours together composing and laying down the tracks.

I wanted the song lyrics to include both English and some of the main African languages: isiXhosa, isiZulu and others. We called the song "Hola Banyana", which loosely translates as 'Celebrate girls'. We then got in a great singer to put down the vocal track.

It was a massive hit at the games. For about three years or more it was played at every SASOL competition and Banyana Banyana match, sometimes continuously throughout the tournaments, until we were all humming the catchy tune in our sleep.

> When you see the Queens of Diski, what are you gonna say?
> Hola Banyana! Hola Banyana! Hola Banyana!
> Banyana bagotsi
> Women are deadly on the ball
> Hola Banyana! Hola Banyana! Hola Banyana!
> Banyana bagotsi

> Liphumile iqembu lezingane, izingane zathatha umhlaba wonke
> *The girls' squad is out, the team taking on the world*
> Zidlubhedu yini? Zishukumisa umzansi
> *Aren't they winning? Aren't they champions? Shaking the Southern Africans*

FRAN HILTON-SMITH

Who's that girl, as skilful as she can be
She's a South African girl
Umethatha lelobhola, uzogcwala
When she takes that ball, you'll be mesmerised

Banyana Banyana, reaching new frontiers, yes
Banyana Banyana join our team
Banyana Banyana empowering, inspiring
Banyana Banyana, Banyana Banyana

Hola Banyana! Hola Banyana! Hola Banyana!
Banyana bagotsi
Hola Banyana! Hola Banyana! Hola Banyana!
Banyana bagotsi

Tlalibone Banyana banyana
Come and see Banyana Banyana
Tlalibone
Who's that girl? She's a defender
Who's that girl? She's a striker
Who's that girl? She's a wing
Who's that girl? She's a centre
Who's that girl? She's a goalkeeper
Who's that girl? A goal-getter

Hola Banyana! Hola Banyana! Hola Banyana!
Banyana bagotsi
Hola Banyana! Hola Banyana! Hola Banyana!
Banyana bagotsi

When you see the Queens of Diski dribbling, what are you gonna say? Who's that girl?
When you see the Queens of Diski diving, what are you gonna say? Who's that girl?
When you see the Queens of Diski flying, what are you gonna say? Who's that girl?
When you see the Queens of Diski scoring, what are you gonna say? Who's that girl?

JOIN FIFA, SEE THE WORLD

Who are Banyana Banyana if not the queens of the football world
South African ambassadors, straight flair, hearts of gold
Hold their heads up high to the sky as they fly on and off the field
All nations to them yield
Masters of skill and speed uniting a nation of varying creeds

Siyanibongela *(congratulations)*! True African queens
Banyana Banyana fly our flag ngokukhanya *(with light)*
World-class athletes, our mothers, daughters, sisters
We're watching with pride in our hearts, you always try
Banyana Banyana the name lives on, will never die
Banyana Banyana the spirit lives on, will never die

Banyana Banyana, reaching new frontiers, yes
Banyana Banyana join our team
Banyana Banyana empowering, inspiring
Banyana Banyana, Banyana Banyana

We charged SASOL a R20,000 fee to write and record the song, which in retrospect was a steal for them considering the impact it had. Leon and I weren't really thinking about payment because we were having such a good time in the studio.

Later, SASOL suggested we write and record a follow-up song. Leon and I soon got down to it, but before we could finish recording, a new broom arrived in the SASOL marketing department who wanted his friends to write and perform the track. I was particularly disappointed not only for creative reasons but also because I had already paid the singer out of my pocket. The other group charged in excess of R120,000. SAFA refused to pay, so the group got in lawyers to fight their case. They got no sympathy from me. The new song never took off like "Hola Banyana", which until recently was still being played at games.

I continued to coach junior coaches and future instructors throughout Africa for CAF and COSAFA. These were the women who would lead the game in the years to come. The courses were draining, not least because of all the travelling around the lesser known parts of the continent, but I like to think I was earning some respect from my colleagues in both CAF and FIFA. Notwithstanding the occasional below par accommodation, I was certainly treated well. At the time of writing I am the only woman and only South African to have ever served on the CAF Technical Committee for three successive terms.

I had to fit all these extra responsibilities around my day job at SAFA: national teams manager. Although no longer coach, I had to accept my share of responsibility to improve the teams' results, which were not exactly what they should have been.

Then we got a breakthrough. Banyana Banyana qualified for the 2012 London Olympics after we beat Ethiopia 4–1 on aggregate in the deciding match. And we wouldn't be alone. For the first time the Olympics allowed two nations from the continent, the other being Cameroon.

The world of women's football was growing: sponsorships, attendance, TV rights, and all the public attention that came with it. The big players in international football were not from Africa, so for expert guidance we had to look overseas. It was clear to me that we needed an experienced European or American coach to develop our talent and get close to our potential. In Europe, national teams play each other regularly, so they are constantly honing skills and learning new tactics. Their coaches had proven skills as brilliant tacticians that ensured they stayed ahead of the advancing pack. South African players—both male and female—were initially wary of innovative tactics because they were not exposed to them. It was apparent to anyone who took even a cursory interest that our best coaches were ex-players who had plied their trade in Europe for many years: Pitso Mosimane, Steve Kompela, Jomo Sono, Eric Tinkler and Benni McCarthy among them.

In preparation for the Olympics I recruited a world champion coach from Germany, Tina Theune, who had previously come out to help me and had proven herself to be beyond brilliant. I was sure that as technical advisor she would make a great 'right-hand woman' for the coach, Joseph Mkhonza. It was quite a coup because the German soccer federation offered to pay her expenses, which included flying her back and forth to Europe. As she was about to board the plane in Germany, Mkhonza and his new assistant Jerry Laka—with not a whiff of big tournament experience between them—decided that they, and they alone, would prepare the team for the Olympics and told her not to come. I was bitterly disappointed that we would not make use of such a golden opportunity to learn from one of the world's great female coaches, not to mention the waste of SAFA money that had already been spent in preparation for her arrival.

Joseph and Jerry must still have been smarting from the power struggle over Tina Theune's role because I was denied a ticket to attend the Olympics, which broke my heart. We had finally fought our way through to a world-class tournament but I had to be content with watching it on TV at home. In the group stage we lost to both Sweden (4–1) and Canada (3–0) before scraping a point in a goalless draw against Japan, but at least for the first time we could now call ourselves Olympians.

The excitement of being at the tournament couldn't disguise the team's disappointment that we could have performed a lot better with some quality coaching. Following a number of losses, the new SAFA president Danny Jordaan terminated Mkhonza's contract. He said the team was making the same mistakes over and over again. For once I had to agree with him.

Two years later, in 2014, I managed to talk former Netherlands head coach Vera Pauw into coming to South Africa to assist us. I had worked with her for a number of years at FIFA and I thought she would be perfect for the job. Even though this time the European coach was allowed to come, unfortunately the appointment would barely last a year. Vera offered insightful tactical input and tried hard to create a robust squad. She was clear about her tactics and the players knew what was required of them. If only sport were that simple.

Some of the team took exception to her unequivocal training methods and tactical approaches and consequently dragged their feet, literally. There were also some cultural issues at play that were never fully resolved. We then played the African Women's Championship in Namibia and lost badly to teams we had previously beaten in friendlies. Soon after failing to qualify for the 2015 World Cup in Canada, Vera left. Former captain Desiree Ellis, who had acted as her assistant, took the helm.

Despite the poor results on the field, there was some good news. Our striker Portia Modise won the 2014 South African Sports Star of the Year award. On the Sandton Convention Centre stage in front of thousands, she was presented with her award together with a new BMW and R1 million cash. Not knowing I was sitting in the audience, she held up the keys, and said, 'Fran, you can take the car for a test drive!'

We then qualified for the 2016 Rio Olympics and repeated our disappointing performance in London, losing to both Sweden (1–0) and China (2–0) and scraping a point against Brazil in a goalless draw. The team returned home from an Olympic Games once again without having found the back of the net.

JOIN FIFA, SEE THE WORLD

The lesson learned from Vera's tenure at Banyana Banyana was that if some influential players either did not like or harboured a grudge against the coach, they had the power to influence the other players not to perform. It is known amongst coaches in the trade as 'losing the dressing room'. Some players, often due to petty rivalries or perceived slights, refused to see the big picture, and the team suffered. I believe this cost us World Cup qualification on two occasions when we should have easily reached the finals.

The first time I noticed this reluctance to play was in a game against Ghana at AFCON 1998, while Augustine Makalakalane was coach. It was also a World Cup qualifying year, which meant that in our final match we only had to draw to qualify for the 1999 World Cup. One striker had over fifty (50!) shots on target and missed every one. We were heading for a 0–0 draw, and looked like we would scrape into the finals despite the underwhelming performance. Then disaster struck. In the final minutes on a wet pitch, a Ghanaian striker advanced on goal. As she got in the 18-yard box she lost control and the ball headed for the back line; simultaneously our goalkeeper had come out, slipped on the greasy pitch and brought the player down. Penalty! We lost 1–0 and the Black Queens went off to their first World Cup in the USA. I was heartbroken. In the post-match meeting the player who had difficulty finding the back of the net said she didn't want to win the game if it meant going to the World Cup with Makalakalane. I have never understood the logic, but then again I never understood the full extent of the personal animosities that festered within the squad.

The same happened at the 2015 World Cup qualifiers in Namibia. Banyana Banyana, led by Vera Pauw, had previously beaten Cameroon, Ivory Coast and others in friendlies by big scores—4–1; 4–0—but in Namibia lost to them all, which meant no World Cup in Canada. We had it in our hands and threw it away. I later learned that some players simply did not want the Dutch coach to lead us to the World Cup. Talk about cutting your nose to spite your face.

With other members of the FIFA organising committee, I was appointed as match commissioner to some international games. The new role required less work than the Technical Study Group, and meant being in charge of the pre-match meetings in which we would discuss the upcoming game and plan logistical matters such as checking the kits did not clash. Later I would write a report about the game, including comments about the referee's and assistant referees' performances, any exceptional circumstances such as poor sportsmanship, crowd violence, disturbances or extreme weather, etc.

In this role I visited Russia to cover the under-20s tournament, then again in Chile in 2008 and Japan in 2012. I was a member of the organising committee for Canada 2014 and Papua New Guinea in 2016. I was clocking up more air miles than Richard Branson.

These trips were not only beneficial to the future of women's football in South Africa, they were also personal travel highlights that will stay with me forever. All work and no play makes Fran a dull girl! For instance, I wrote the first under-17 Women's World Cup technical report in Japan in 2008. It was a place about which I would never normally have been curious but once there I could appreciate the country's beauty and the courteousness of its people. I lived for a glorious month in Tokyo's Conrad Hotel next to the Japanese Princess Gardens where I spent many happy hours walking.

In between all the FIFA responsibilities I was still delivering instructors' courses, some of which were closer to home. I was sent to African countries where women were both eager to learn new skills and desperate to join the international family of women's football. It was on a FIFA trip to Nigeria that I got to know the people better and appreciated their culture on a deeper level, as opposed to being sent on magical mystery tours in the bush.

I also continued my duties as part of the FIFA Technical Study Group at the Japan and Russia World Cups; then back to the USA twice and Canada once more. I enjoyed the travel, the responsibility, and the feeling that I was a small but important cog in the FIFA machine that was helping women's football thrive. FIFA officials always gave me the impression that they were glad they had found someone who was willing to fly to all these places and provide detailed reports on the tournaments. But actually it felt like I was finally being appreciated for my battles during the frustrating years at SAFA.

My trips overseas also had a profound impact on my professional outlook. I learnt so much about team tactics, match preparation, personal fitness, player management, nutrition and every other aspect of elite sport during these international forays. I like to think that my beloved Banyana Banyana benefited from that knowledge on my return. However, talking about my travels to the World Cup was not like experiencing it. I would have to wait many more years before Banyana Banyana joined the family of nations at the top table and played in a World Cup.

Whenever I visited FIFA's Zürich offices I would brag about the South African players, comparing them to some of the best in the world. My confidence was born of natural optimism and a large dose of blind faith, realising that if I didn't believe in the future of South African football no one else would. The foreign delegates, fully aware of our poor-to-middling results in the mid-2000s throughout Africa, would roll their eyes and think that I was just being a crazy patriot. South Africa was a long way from being able to compete on the world stage.

But that was then. My bragging was enough to pique the interest of European teams to come out and play us in Cape Town: Sweden (twice) and the Netherlands (three times). These international friendlies were a regular fixture in the men's game but not so in the women's; playing against these fine European sides kept us in touching distance of the elite and reminded us how far we had come on the road marked "World Cup".

In August 2015 FIFA formed a task force made up of representatives from each confederation to discuss the way forward for women's football. This was in response to calls for action made at the earlier women's symposium prior to the World Cup in Canada that year. Little old Fran was asked to represent Africa. What an honour. The task force, chaired by Moya Dodd, held meetings in Zürich and made recommendations to the FIFA reform committee. It was a long way to go for a simple sit-down but it was worth it because I found the meetings both instructive and inspiring, and felt that we had the power in our hands to bring a lot of positive change to the women's game.

The committee was considering topics that had been of interest to me for years: a desire to get more women coaches into the national teams; to ensure at least half of the technical staff were women (at my instigation South Africa had already implemented this); and to get more women appointed in leading administrative roles in the national federations. These were lofty aims that were certainly not easy to implement in Africa, but we made a promising start when FIFA adopted one of these policies for the upcoming under-17s Women's World Cup, where there would be at least one woman coach on the bench.

This was Sepp Blatter's last year as president and he would occasionally attend the meetings to catch up on our progress. I was always amazed that he would take the time to meet us considering the fraught year he was undergoing. He was being investigated for dubious payments to UEFA boss Michel Platini. It didn't end well for him. In December 2015, following years of controversy, FIFA's ethics committee banned both Blatter and Platini from football for eight years, later reduced to six.

Despite all the allegations and findings against him, it is fair to say that Blatter was a keen supporter of the women's game. He was replaced by Gianni Infantino, who brought in sweeping changes and pushed out many old hands, including my long-time boss and head of women's football Tatjana Haeni. She was replaced by New Zealander Sarai Bareman who implemented fresh plans and ideas.

One of the new initiatives was the FIFA Female Leadership Development programme, a great project that saw the 211 associations around the world appoint women candidates for the FIFA courses, to be trained as future leaders and role models. I was excited to be appointed as one of the mentors for the programme and had three women assigned to me for workshops in the Netherlands, Switzerland and Canada. Many on the programme went on to lead women's football in their respective countries. I kept in touch with the African mentees and still assist them where I can.

The previous year, 2014, I was sent once again to one of my favourite destinations, Canada, to report on the under-20 Women's World Cup, this time based in Montreal. I went as a member of the FIFA organising committee, so was relieved of too much match reporting. One game was in Toronto, a short flight away. On arrival, my colleague Moya Dodd (an Aussie), who had been on the same flight, was met by a chauffeur-driven limo. She was on the FIFA Exco, one of the first women to serve, so was treated like royalty. She offered me a lift to the hotel which I gleefully accepted. On the journey we saw signs for Niagara Falls. I have always been obsessed with waterfalls and of course had already seen Victoria Falls on the Zambia/Zimbabwe border a number of times. I suggested to Moya we go see them. She agreed. What an experience.

A combination of guilt that Dara back home was missing out on this wonderful experience and wanting to share it with her, made me call and tell her to immediately book a flight for Montreal. On my day off we both flew back to Toronto to see the falls with my cousin, who later put us up at her place.

Another particularly memorable time shared with Dara was when I had to fly to Zürich during winter for a FIFA meeting. Everyone was complaining about the weather but we both loved it when the air filled with big puffy snowflakes, always a joyous moment for a South African. We booked ourselves onto the highest mountain railway in the Alps, the Bernina Express from Zermatt to St Moritz with stunning views of the Matterhorn. Dara was always on the lookout for a discount and, boy, this time she hit the jackpot when she cut out a discount voucher in a promotional flyer for an upgrade to first class. We paid for two economy tickets and handed the conductor the voucher. He had not seen one before and was more than a bit dubious, and in any case he thought the first class carriage was full. He checked and there were two seats available, so now he couldn't refuse us. We were soon mixing with Swiss high society in opulent leather armchairs sipping champagne while looking out through the glass ceiling at the snowy fairytale scenery of cabins, goats and chalets all the way to the Matterhorn. I could almost hear someone singing tunes from *The Sound of Music*.

We continued the trip by luxury coach down to Lugano and Lake Como in Italy and slept over in a magnificent old house. Something as simple as walking down to the old town and sharing a huge pizza with wine made life seem perfect. It *was* perfect.

The final overseas jol for Dara and I was another trip to Canada. I was based in Vancouver, home of my friend Metro Gerela. I mentioned to Metro that Dara harboured a dream of visiting Alaska, a relatively short voyage from our base. He called an acquaintance who ran one of the biggest Alaskan cruise lines and helped us book a beautiful cabin with balcony and arranged some of his Italian mates to meet us at the harbour to carry our luggage onboard. Other passengers must have thought we were celebrities. Well, we felt like it. We wallowed in seven days of pure luxury on the ocean waves on a ship which was more like a floating hotel. Join FIFA and see the world.

The highlight of the trip was seeing the Hubbard Glacier, an intensely beautiful blue wall of ice 122 kilometres long and 183 metres high. We were bundled up in thick coats and scarves with woolly caps on deck while fellow guests swam in the heated pools and lounged in jacuzzis. The glacier was disintegrating, evidence of which we could see in the huge blocks of ice that silently floated past the ship.

We then took a helicopter flight, which landed on a glacier. We were given big puffy spiked boots that ensured we didn't slip on the ice, and made us look like a couple of Michelin men. I was a bit nervous as there were deep cracks underneath my feet with water streaming below but Dara happily wandered around the glacier.

I loved sharing these trips with Dara who not only appreciated the international travel but also the quality of international football at the games. From those dark days of working unpaid as the manager of the women's national team, she had later worked as a medical rep before moving on to the sports goods manufacturing company Reebok as their football and rugby category manager. From there she was taken on by footballing giants Kaizer Chiefs in 2005 and has been their brand manager ever since. Dara has been as closely involved in football as I have, and we have shared many profound footballing and personal moments over the years. And so it made perfect sense that in 2018 I asked her to marry me. She said yes, and we planned to make our relationship legally permanent with a civil union. Thirty-one years after meeting, we finally decided to 'jump the broom' together!

We wanted a small event with no fuss with Dara's close friend Sandy as her witness and my child Carla as mine. Dara's sister Olive was overseas so it would have been unfair to ask my sister Lynda to stand witness if hers could not attend. We found a White Robed Catholic Church bishop who agreed to perform the service, because a gay wedding was unheard of in the traditional Catholic church, and still is. Maybe one day.

The bishop had constructed a lovely wooden chapel in his garden, which would make a beautiful setting for the ceremony, after which we would go back to our friends Sandy and Jani's stunning mountain home for the reception. I booked a pink Cadillac stretch limo for the day.

Out of the blue, once Dara's sister Olive heard about the wedding she decided to come over from England for the ceremony where she could join my sister, Carla, niece Leigh and nephew Brett and his fiancée Ruth.

So much for the wedding plans. A few days before the wedding Dara developed bronchopneumonia. She became seriously ill and I had to rush her to hospital where she had an operation to drain an abscess. I was worried sick. Now we had to consider postponing the ceremony, but her sister had already booked the flight. It was touch and go—should we cancel the wedding or go ahead despite Dara's frail condition.

As the big day drew closer we kept asking the doctor if she could be safely discharged from hospital. After much begging, at the last minute the doctor agreed to release her the day before the wedding. Sandy fetched Dara from the hospital while I fetched Olive from the airport. It was that tight. To compound Dara's pain, on her arrival home in the SUV she somehow managed to pull a muscle in her stomach as she got out of the car. In retrospect, considering the pain she went through, Dara probably should have remained in hospital instead of taking the journey home.

Next morning, ceremony day, Dara could not get out of bed from all the ailments she was now accruing. Disaster loomed. She could not even get on her feet, so we arranged a wheelchair. But how were we going to get her to the bishop's garden? We could not postpone the event because of all the food and other arrangements that had been made. If we can't go to him, we thought, could he come to us? He agreed.

We cancelled the limo and brought all the food and paraphernalia from Sandy and Jani's place. Olive helped dress Dara in a lovely outfit she had sent from England. (I wore a grey outfit and blue veldskoens!) Then everyone pitched in to set up tables and chairs in the garden. We arranged a makeshift altar, which wasn't exactly the Cathedral of Christ the King but it did the job. Sandy, Ruth, Olive and Leigh hung sparkling crystals and ornaments everywhere, and with the altar placed on the edge of the lawn it looked like a fairyland in the bright sunshine of Hazeldene.

Sandy and I had spent many days choosing the songs for the ceremony. I wanted the Elvis Costello version of "She"; Dara liked Dolly Parton's "I Will Always Love You".

But we had not listened closely to the lyrics. When I had earlier asked Dara to name her favourite songs she had no idea it was for the wedding, so did not realise how unsuitable a sad song about lost love would be. Woops. Dara only told me as I was writing this chapter.

The music we loved when we got together had been by a rock band called Survivor, so we played "I Cant Hold Back" and "The Search is Over". For my speech I read out the words of the Bee Gees song "To Love Somebody". Everybody cried. The only response to that was to break out the booze and get stuck into some of Jani's delicious food.

Olive, Ruth, Leigh, Lynda, Brett, Sandy and Jani worked miracles that day and I thank them all for making it memorable for Dara and me.

14

DOING IT FOR OURSELVES

Writing a memoir of one's life and times necessarily makes it sound as if you are blowing your own trumpet a little too loudly and perhaps laying on your achievements a bit thick. I don't wish to create the impression that I was the only woman fighting for women's rights or making a difference within the game. Nothing could be further from the truth. If I've enjoyed a special life, it has in large part been due to a combination of happy accidents and wonderful friends and colleagues that I met along the way. Likewise, I hope the (mostly) women I have helped during my career see me as being generous with my time and knowledge.

There are plenty of women whose brains I picked, whose advice I took, and whose expertise I valued, not least of which are many international contemporaries and colleagues. I camped for a while with the US women's national team where I learned first-hand from former World Cup-winning player and coach April Heinrich, and later in Germany with World Cup-winning coach Tina Theune. I took courses with national coaches Vera Pauw (Banyana), Sylvie Béliveau (Canada), Marika Domanski-Lyfors (Sweden), Hope Powell (England), Carolina Morace (Italy and Brazil), Anne Noe (Belgium), and of course my ever patient FIFA boss and friend Tatjana Haeni.

Fortunately, thanks to invitations from FIFA and CAF, I also got to mingle with some of the top male coaches in the world, such as Ghanaian legends Charles Gyamfi and Ben Koufie, Bafana coaching genius Carlos Quieroz, Stuart Baxter, Shakes Mashaba, Ted Dumitru and Farouk Khan, to name a few.

Closer to home I got lots of support from current Bafana Bafana coach Molefi Ntseki, Thabo Senong, Alex Heredia, Cameron Cox and Steve Coetzee. My thanks is due them and many others because their encouragement and occasional scepticism kept me motivated enough to drag our nation's three women's teams onto the world stage.

In particular there were two driven South Africans who brought vigour to their respective roles and energised everything they touched. They not only helped the game but also assisted me in different ways, so it is appropriate that I put my thanks on record.

Firstly, Anastasia Tsichlas, (Nastasia or Nat as I call her). She and I rose up the ranks at both CAF and FIFA at a similar time, but on different paths—she more in administration, me in coaching. From 1982 she sat on the executive committee of the National Soccer League, was the first woman elected to the PSL executive, the first chairperson of the women's football committee, chairperson of the indoor football committee, competitions committee, SAFA international board, and served on the FIFA 2010 World Cup marketing and legacy committees. You could say she was well connected. It's a wonder she had any time left to actually watch a game.

As managing director of the Mamelodi Sundowns she led one of only two South African clubs to have won the CAF Champions League.

There were apartheid-era rumours that she, together with black administrators and club owners, drove around the townships in the dead of night plotting and planning for the time sport would be de-politicised. I believe the top guys in the game such as Irvin Khosa and Kaizer Motaung still respect her for that.

In 1990 she and her husband bought the Sundowns in conjunction with the wealthy Krok brothers. The club kept winning trophies, more than any other team in SA Premier League history. Without a doubt they were the best team of the 1990s. They sold the club in 2004.

I hope Nat will forgive me for saying that she had two sides to her personality. She could be a fiery dragon one minute and then turn around and be kindness personified. I had experience with both characters, which was sometimes hard work. I often went for months when she would not talk to me for some silly reason or other; then she would phone me out of the blue as if nothing had happened. Having said that, she was a great advocate for Banyana Banyana, and even once came with us to Nigeria as a member of the travelling party and cooked a meal for the players! She also helped me get Vera Pauw to South Africa by putting a word in the ear of those who made such decisions, notably Danny Jordaan.

Another dynamo in the world of women's football is Ria Ledwaba, a more even-tempered lady who rarely gets worked up. She came from a football family of four brothers, and grew to love the game. She started a boy's team in the Chappies-sponsored little league in the late

1980s. In 1989 she founded the professional team Ria Stars, which reached the PSL in 2000. But it was hard to run a PSL team in the early days without a big sponsor—she once told me that on match days she would count the spectators coming into the stadium to see if she would be able to cover her costs for the game. Normally the take on the gate fell short. After a number of years she sold the club.

Our paths crossed often. Ria led the administration responsibilities of the HPC in 2002 and later managed the programme, and was instrumental in getting the National Lotteries Commission to assist with funding. She later joined the SAFA NEC.

Ria, who till then had supported Danny Jordaan as SAFA president, started requesting details of all the funding that came to the organisation. When she got no satisfactory answer she contacted the Minister of Sport. The result? She was suspended, but won an appeal and they had to reinstate her. Ria deserves her place on the NEC, and not merely because she is one of only six women on the board of thirty-six members.

The year 2018 was not only memorable for affirming my domestic arrangements, it also gave Banyana Banyana another chance to prove themselves at the African Women's Championship, now renamed Africa Women Cup of Nations, in Ghana. The championship would also act as qualification (for the two finalists and the third place team) to take the three coveted spots in the 2019 World Cup in France.

I was not allowed to travel with the team, but considering our recent results and the potential of the squad, I believed we were destined for great things in Ghana. I *had* to be there. Consequently I managed to get myself appointed onto the CAF Technical Study Group for the tournament. I was based in Cape Coast, a relaxed town with pristine beaches on which fishermen returned every evening with their catch in old wooden canoes, like a scene from a bygone era. Banyana Banyana played their group games 150 kilometres along the coast in the capital, Accra.

In the first game we faced long-time foes Nigeria. I spent the first eighty-four minutes of the match in front of the TV set with a tight knot in my stomach until Thembi Kgatlana scored in the 85th. Rather than relax and enjoy the moment, the knot got tighter and my heart raced; now we had to hang on for the final whistle. The team played out the remaining minutes like professionals and won the game 1–0.

Next, we faced another old foe: Equatorial Guinea. But they were not as strong as the Super Falcons and we dispatched them 7–1.

The final group stage match was against Zambia. Hero of the Nigeria match Kgatlana scored for Banyana in the 8th minute, but Zambia equalized in the 10th. A draw would put us through to the semis on goal difference. I sweated out the next eighty minutes as I did the Nigeria match. But we held on. We were through to the semi-final against Mali with the promise of a place in the following year's World Cup.

In Accra, Nigeria played Cameroon for a place in the final. Meanwhile the South Africa v Mali semi-final would be played in Cape Coast, so I could attend the game, potentially the most important in Banyana's history.

What a game. The new Cape Coast Sports Stadium was packed with a sizeable contingent from South Africa and all the top brass from CAF. Some matches seem to drag on but this one flew by in a blur. *Les Aiglonnes* (the Female Eagles) were no pushover, but we scored first with a Kgatlana strike before Ramalepe made it 2–0. We held on for the last nine minutes to record a memorable victory. The final whistle blew and the whole stadium erupted. All the South African support staff who were sitting in seats below me started jumping about and hugging each other, something I dearly wanted to do but, as an impartial CAF official, I had to sit in silence and behave with decorum. Inside, though, I was going crazy and was flooded with emotions. I had put everything I had into football during the past twenty years, believing, trusting, hoping for this moment. And here it was… a 2–0 win over Mali was sending us to France 2019.

World Cup here we come. The result confirmed Des Ellis as the most successful women's coach in South African football. She won the CAF Women's Coach of the Year award twice, in 2018 and 2019, and led the winning Banyana Banyana side to the southern Africa COSAFA title four years in a row. Now she would lead them to the World Cup.

Even though we had accomplished the long-term goal, our tournament was not yet over. We still had to play the final against Nigeria who had beaten Cameroon in the other semi-final. With an ominous feeling of déjà vu, we faced our old enemy once more. But it somehow felt different because we had already beaten them in the first match of the tournament. Perhaps the Super Falcons' spell over us had been broken and this would be our year. Following the euphoria of beating Mali, it would be difficult to lift the girls once more to produce another Herculean effort on the field.

The final was a tough end to end game with neither side giving an inch. After ninety minutes it was 0–0. Penalties! We lost 4–3.

It was a bittersweet result, but what a consolation prize! France here we come.

I sat in the stadium in silence but with my heart bursting with pride and wanting to share the moment with someone. Dreams do come true.

DOING IT FOR OURSELVES

There was one more reason to be happy. Our star striker Thembi Kgatlana was the top goalscorer and voted best player of the tournament. I couldn't agree more.

When Danny Jordaan took over the SAFA presidency in 2013, it signalled a change of fortunes for many people—mine took a nosedive. In fact, I'm surprised I lasted another six years. I guess I kept my head down.

During that time I was running women's football as general manager (no additional money), then acted as technical director for two and a half years (no extra money) and then took a demotion to assistant technical director (ditto). I also ran the High Performance Centre for, you guessed it, sweet FA. I never received a cent for all the extra jobs I did. After I left I heard through the grapevine that men in similar senior roles earned far more than me.

Then, in May 2019, after twenty years of loyal service, in his great wisdom Jordaan used the excuse that I was too old for the job and retired me off, ostensibly because I had reached the age of sixty (in fact I was sixty-six). Neither he nor chief executive Russell Paul were man enough to tell me face to face, so they asked Neil Tovey, then technical director, to dispense the bad news. I was stunned. I could tell Neil was both disappointed and embarrassed by the whole affair. I was embarrassed for *him* having to do someone else's dirty work.

I asked when I was expected to vacate the place because I was in the middle of some big women's projects for which I had received millions of rands in funding from FIFA and the Department of Sport and Recreation. 'At the end of the month,' said Neil. It was a shocking blow, not only because it was a complete surprise but also because it was just a month before France 2019. I faced the prospect of Banyana Banyana going to the World Cup without me.

I was told to take two months paid leave that was due, but of course, silly me, being as dedicated as I am, I came into the office and tried to hand over the projects to other people. But really, who actually cared?

I often wonder what was the final straw that led to what was effectively my summary dismissal. I can only guess. Jordaan and I never saw eye to eye (frankly, he never liked me, for undisclosed reasons) and I believe he was jealous that I was accepted and respected by FIFA. He was rude to me at every opportunity, and once screamed that he would fire me for no reason at all, a not uncommon event. His style of 'leadership' consisted of shouting a lot and trying to intimidate people. He may have been the big cheese in SAFA but he had his own run-in with FIFA over the 2015 corruption case when he admitted paying $10 million to Jack Warner, the head of the Americas confederation in the run-up to the 2012 World Cup. This money was supposedly for the African diaspora in Trinidad and Tobago. Despite his unpopularity, no one seemed able to challenge his power; he remains in post as I write. But for how much longer?

During my time in football I was thrilled to receive many presidential and ministerial awards in South Africa and the recognition of my peers around the world, but precious little from our own SAFA. No president or CEO past or present ever thanked me for my efforts to develop women's football or congratulated me for my achievements with FIFA and CAF, where I was regularly acknowledged and felt valued. I must have been doing something right.

Possibly more heartbreaking for me than losing my job and the lack of approbation was Jordaan's decision to refuse permission for me to travel with Banyana Banyana to the two Olympic Games in London and Rio. I had been allowed to go on the London site inspection, but when it came to the actual games he refused. Same for Rio.

Even worse was the way I was treated in the run-up to Banyana Banyana's first ever World Cup in France, 2019. Except for the inaugural World Cup in 1991, I had never missed a tournament. Now my dream was about to come true at the very moment I was sent into exile, I mean retirement. My whole life I had waited for this moment, ever since I scrimped and saved to attend the 1995 tournament in Sweden and later in the USA 1999 and 2003, China 2007, Germany 2011 and Canada 2015. For years my dream of Banyana Banyana reaching the World Cup had been all I talked about to anyone who would listen. Everyone in football knew what it meant to me. That included Jordaan. I kept asking the acting CEO, Russel Paul, if he would agree to my inclusion in the delegation, but he kept putting me off, saying he was waiting for the president's approval. After stringing me along for two weeks before the tournament, the answer came back: No.

It was destined to be the first World Cup I would miss since 1995—and Banyana Banyana were playing in it! After all I had put into the teams, to be treated so heartlessly illustrated the kind of person Jordaan was. I felt as though something precious was being taken away from me and I found it difficult to control my reaction to such a snub. I had to keep my lips sealed for fear of what I might say.

But then I was offered a lifeline. FIFA invited me to attend the Women's Symposium in Paris prior to the tournament, which included a free flight and a ticket to Banyana's first group game. I would be there after all. I arranged and paid for my own accommodation and travel for the next two group stage matches (not cheap in France) and between FIFA and my SAFA colleagues, I rustled up VVIP tickets to the games. I was hardly bereft of friends, but as you can guess I didn't spend much time hobnobbing with Jordaan and his cronies in the VVIP lounge.

It was great to bear witness to the success of reaching the finals, but it has to be said that Banyana Banyana did not play to their potential. We struggled against strong opposition, losing all three group stage games: against China 1–0; Germany 4–0; and Spain 3–1 (in which Thembi Kgatlana can go down in the record books as the first South African to score in a World Cup tournament).

After the game against Spain, Jordaan and I had a few unpleasant words about the reasons why the team had lost. As he hardly spoke to me without being rude, I wished he had rather kept quiet.

On a personal level the pressures of football took its toll on my physical and mental health, especially during my time at the South African Football Association. I firmly believe most of my ailments were caused, or at least exacerbated, by the immense stress of my job. I was forever fighting at SAFA for every little thing—trying to build women's football with people who were doing their best to ignore me and ridicule my ideas, hoping I would go away.

Also, commitment often means paying a price in one's personal relationships. Football was such a big part of my life that I was not present to witness either my father's or my mother's passing on. In 2008 my father was admitted to hospital shortly after I had left for Equatorial Guinea for the African Women's Championships. He passed on three days later, on 18 November. SAFA CEO Raymond Hack kindly offered to fly me back but I felt I couldn't leave the team. My dad was gone, I could do nothing about it, so when we laid him to rest was not crucial. I had a job to do so stayed with my team.

My mom passed away in 2016 when I was at a FIFA meeting in Zürich. She had broken her back after a fall, and I was lucky to be able to comfort her in hospital before I left for Switzerland. In effect I was saying goodbye. Looking at the doctors' reports I feared that there was no chance of a full recovery. When I returned two days later, my sister Lynda and I rushed to the hospital. A staff member broke the news that Mom had passed. Even if she had recovered to some degree, she would never have been happy as an invalid. She died on my brother Brendan's birthday, 15 March. I think she decided to check out on her son's birthday, the boy she had loved so dearly and lost so young.

However I can't blame all my physical ailments on football. All those years of judo, karate and rowing caught up with me in later life. I was diagnosed with rheumatoid arthritis and subjected to weekly injections with powerful drugs, before another specialist told me I was in fact suffering from *osteo*arthritis, which required completely different treatment. Doctors! Then I was diagnosed with haemochromatosis (iron overload), for which I had blood siphoned off once a month. Both my knees have been replaced and my spine had to be fused due to a combination of degeneration of the cartilage and worsening arthritis.

As I have already mentioned, two fingers of my right hand had already been fused, so it has been an age since I picked up a guitar. I also badly broke my right ankle when I slipped on a newly polished floor at the SAFA offices. I still have a steel plate, a bolt and seven screws inside me to show for it. I should have sued them for the workplace injury. My friend and goalkeeper coach Alex Heredia used to call me Robocoach for good reason.

Consequently I had to sell the motorbike to my brother-in-law and biking buddy Billy as I was scared I would not be able to hold it upright anymore—or pick it up if I dropped it. I am always filled with envy whenever Harley Low Riders roar past and I am sorely tempted to splash out on a new bike. But having come to terms with my physical limitations and after Billy passed away in 2014, my wind-in-the-hair days are a thing of the past. From running like the wind on the left wing as a soccer player to battling to walk upstairs, my life has changed irrevocably.

Despite the personal cost, I believe I have made a difference to the women's game, and I'm not finished yet. I am still contacted by coaches and administrators—both men and women—for guidance, and to lead courses for them, as long as it is not too physically taxing.

I hope the results speak for themselves and made all the sacrifices worthwhile. I helped the senior women's team qualify for two Olympic Games and a World Cup, and we made it to two under-17 World Cups. I encouraged and mentored twenty-seven CAF A licence female coaches and eighty-seven FIFA-qualified administrators in all fifty-three regions of SAFA. This empowerment of black women in sport is the greatest gift I can give to the next generation. I am proud that in some small way I have left a legacy of confident women who can take the game forward.

Another great success was the High Performance Centre in Pretoria that provided skills training and education to girls who have made the most of the opportunity—just look at the number of South African professionals now playing for foreign clubs who got their start at the HPC, and how many received university degrees thanks to football. Who would have thought it.

Now, as my coaching responsibilities diminish, I look to those keen young women who, like me all those years ago, can bring their own brand of enthusiasm to the beautiful game. We have made a start, now it is up to them to take that self-belief and encourage more women to take a step up the ladder. I have passed the baton on. My race is done.

Hopefully the next generation can be more assertive than I was. My personal weakness was to worry about things too much; consequently I suffered a lot of self-imposed stress. Another weakness was that I put up with too much bullshit from people. I have been too soft for my own good, and not bold enough when it came to making decisions. Let that be a lesson to the next generation.

Perhaps this is a good moment to add a small word of caution for the new women coming through. In my experience it is still too common to see women more prepared to pull each other down than offer a helping hand. It is as if some women are worried that someone else's spotlight will diminish their own. But that is not the case.

Praise is so easy to give, and so motivational, that it surprises me that women don't share it more often. I have found that a small amount of encouragement offered at a crucial time in someone's career or life can have dramatic effects. I know because I've benefitted from it—and passed it on.

I am not blind to the fact that some cultural attitudes are difficult to break. When women in some cultures have been taught to approach their husbands on their knees, it is always going to be a struggle to empower them in the workplace. There is nothing I can do to change the culture of hundreds of years, but I can help boost women's self-confidence, which is the first step to achieving great things.

Wherever you can, sisters, offer each other a helping hand, even though this effort will have to take place in the face of the institutionalised male-dominated glass ceiling... male dominated for no other reason than they had a head start. The success of the women's game in the USA has proved that it can be a money-spinner, bringing paying spectators, big sponsorships and a fair income for players and coaches. Once the money comes into the women's game, respect will follow.

Despite this, women's football in South Africa is still fed the crumbs off the SAFA table, while some NEC members harbour an unhealthy disregard for our game.

Even if Banyana Banyana's success will have to wait, we can at least push individual players to think big. Football can change lives. The inspirational High Performance Centre and the showcase of playing in the World Cup meant that our players got noticed, were then signed by professional clubs, and started earning good money, which brings independence and power.

My dream had paid off—fourteen of our interns have (so far) graduated with university degrees, and many others play for teams around the globe. The roll call of both HPC graduates and national squad players is quite impressive:

- Thembi Kgatlana and Noko Matlou (SD Eibar, Spain; previously Houston Dash, USA)
- Janine van Wyk, Banyana captain 2013–present (Glasgow City, Scotland; previously Houston Dash)
- Linda Motlhalo (Djurgården, Sweden; previously Houston Dash)
- Nothando Vilakazi (EDF Logroño, Spain)
- Refiloe Jane (AC Milan, Italy)
- Jermaine Seoposenwe (Sporting Braga, Portugal)
- Odi Fulutudilu (Åland United, Finland)
- Kholosa Biyana (Sporting Gijón, Spain)
- Amanda Mthandi (CD Badajoz, Spain)
- Lebogoang Ramalepe, Rhoda Mulaudzi and Bambanani Mbane (Dinamo Minsk, Belarus)
- Andisiwe Mgcoyi and Zanele Nhlapo (KFF Mitrovica, Kosovo)
- Leandra Smeda (Familicão, Portugal)
- Nompumelelo Nyandeni (WFC Rossiyanka, Russia)
- Kelso Peskin (Stade Brestois, France)

- Letago Madiba and Rachel Sebati (Faith Vatan Spor, Turkey)
- Nomvula Kgoale (university in the USA)

I am extremely proud of them all. I had always said Africa was a sleeping giant, and now I believe we have awoken. I predict that one day an African team will win the Women's World Cup, and when it happens I hope I shall be in the stands cheering them on.

FRAN HILTON-SMITH
ACHIEVEMENTS & AWARDS

SPORTING
South African rowing champion, ladies coxed 4, 1973
Karate black belt, under Okinawa Aikido, 1974

COACHING
Springbok (SAWFA) football coach, 1991–2
State President's silver medal for contribution to football, 1992
CAF high level coaching course, 1995
English Football Association course, 1995
KNVB Dutch coaching course, 1996
FIFA Futuro 11 course, 1993
South African Students Sports Union (SASSU) national football coach, 1997
U-19 women's national team coach, 1999–2000
Senior women's national team coach, 1999–2000
FIFA instructor, 2001
CAF instructor, 2005–present
CAF A licence, 2012
SAFA Pro licence, 2013
COSAFA instructor, 2019–present
First and only female member of the Confederation of African Football technical committee, 2014–present
FIFA Technical Study Group (u-19 Canada, 2001; u-20 Thailand, 2004; Russia, 2006; senior USA, 2003; China, 2007; New Zealand, 2008; Germany, 2011)

Senior Instructor, CAF online instructors' workshop, 2021
COSAFA leadership project, southern African women administrators, 2021

ADMINISTRATION
President of South African Women's Football Association (SAWFA), 1991–4
Director, Kalamazoo Foundation for Sport and Education, 1996
Manager, SAFA women's national teams, 1999–2015
Assistant technical director, 2011
Acting technical director, 2012
Manager/coach under-19 women's national team to mid-2001
National teams manager for both senior team and under-20, 2001–2010
Person responsible for HPC, 2004–retirement
General manager for women's football, 2011–retirement
Acting CEO for one week in May 2013!
Member of FIFA u-20 Women's World Cup organising committee, Japan, 2012 & Canada, 2014
SAFA acting technical director, 2014
Assistant technical director (working to Neil Tovey), 2015
Member of FIFA task force to develop women's football, Switzerland & Canada, 2015
Organised three FIFA administration courses in SA for 87 women administrators, 2016–18
Led the High Performance Centre for 18 years.

AWARDS

City of Germiston Gold Sport award for outstanding achievement in sport, 1995

Shoprite Checkers Woman of the Year award, 1997

Germiston Sports awards, gold medal, 1997

Greater Germiston Sports Coach of the Year award, 1998

State President's Award for Contribution to Sport, 2001

Ekurhuleni Sportswoman of the Year (Provincial award), 2002

Ekurhuleni Sports Administrator of the Year (provincial award), 2013

National Sports award honouring women in sport, 2014

Ekurhuleni Outstanding Sport Administrator (provincial award), 2015

G Sport special recognition award (SA Women's Sports Body), 2015

Ekurhuleni Women in Sport awards, president's award, 2019

South African Sport Award, former Minister of Sport Steve Tshwete Lifetime Achievement award, 2019

EDUCATION

Teachers Diploma, Johannesburg College of Education, 1974

Further Diploma in Education, UNISA, 1989

Higher Diploma in Education, UNISA, 1990

Advanced Diploma in Sports Management, RAU University, 1997

CPSIA information can be obtained
at www.ICGtesting.com
Printed in the USA
BVHW071021200721
612311BV00003B/725